HANBOK
The Art of Korean Clothing
Sunny Yang

HOLLYM
Elizabeth, NJ · SEOUL

HANBOK
The Art of Korean Clothing

Sunny Yang

Copyright © 1997
by Sunny Yang

All rights reserved throughout the world.
No part of this book may be reproduced in any form
without permission in writing from the publisher.

First published in 1997
by Hollym International Corp.
18 Donald Place
Elizabeth, New Jersey 07208 USA.
Tel : (908)353-1655   Fax: (908)353-0255
http://www.hollym.com

Published simultaneously in Korea
by Hollym Corporation; Publishers
6th fl., Core Bldg., 13-13 Kwanchol-dong, Chongno-gu
Seoul 110-111, Korea
Tel : (02)735-7551~4   Fax : (02)730-5149
http://www.hollym.co.kr

ISBN : 1-56591-082-6
Library of Congress Catalog Card Number : 97-71680

Printed in Korea

To my children,
Ella, Steven and his wife Katherine,
whose curiosity and interest
in things about Korea,
rekindled mine — .

Foreword

On a day in November 1996, one of the last beautiful days of an autumn in Seoul, the telephone rang. Sunny Yang. I was pleasantly surprised. We had met via SIWA (Seoul International Women's Association).

At that time Sunny did not know that I have admired her book about Japanese textiles and the *Kimono*, "Textile Art of Japan". It is well written with beautiful pictures and very nicely edited and printed.

I wondered why she phoned me. A big favour, she said. I am pleased and I feel honoured that Sunny asked me to write a foreword of her book, "*HANBOK* - The Art of Korean Clothing."

Sunny must have known that I am interested in Korean culture, which has existed for more than 5000 years.

Because my husband is a diplomat, we have moved around about every 3 or 4 years. In March 1993, we received the message that we were to be sent to Korea that August. At that time I was not well-informed of this country in East Asia. Of course, I knew that the Netherlands participated in the Korean War, and in the 17th century after the discovery of Choson, Hendrik Hamel, the first European, wrote about Korea and introduced it to Europe. Preparing ourselves for our move to Korea, I searched in libraries and book stores in Brussels, where we were living at that time, for insights into our new home country. But information about Korea was meager. Luckily we read an article about an exhibition going on at Antwerp, the European cultural center in 1993, in the northern part of Belgium. We went there immediately and viewed a display of Korea's proud *Koryo* celadon, *Yi* white celadon, and unique paintings. As we were viewing the exhibition, my curiosity of "the Land of the Morning Calm" with its Oriental mystery only increased.

Eventually, we moved from Brussels to live in Korea. For me it was the first time in Asia. I was really looking forward to it. It was a kind of surprise that Seoul is such a huge, modern, and dynamic city. I expected a more Asian atmosphere. I looked for remains of the ancient culture. I did not realized that so much of Korea's rich past was gone through various wars and invasions. Nevertheless, with what is left - the traditional architecture, the Celadon, the *Hanbok* etc. - I was so much impressed that I tried to learn "Hangeul", the Korean language, not only to share social experiences but also to get to know the Korean culture better. However, the English language will be for me the obvious means.

Although Korea has been better known to Europeans ever since the Seoul Summer Olympic Game, there is still extremely little information about Korea. In order to catch up with globalization and the internationalization trend, exchange of information of one's own country is as important as economic development.

Nowadays, old traditions seem to disappear so quickly and dissolve in each other. The globe is becoming more and more one world. However, we should be proud of our long histories. We should try to protect the good aspects of it. The traditional dress is one of those. In the Netherlands, my home country, it is becoming very rare that people wear "klederdracht" (= *Hanbok*). In Korea you also see it seldom. Of course, what was fashion in the past or even some years ago can not be expected to be worn nowadays. However, we should try to find modern ways to keep our traditions alive. Sunny Yang's book "*HANBOK* - The Art of Korean Clothing" will be a very helpful resource, and is certainly a blessing for saving the Korean national dress. It is a book which introduces history and culture with beautiful illustrations. It definitely is a book that must be read by those who want to know about Korea and her culture.

Sabine Bronkhorst
President 1996-97
Seoul International Womens Association

Preface

When westerners think of Korea, what often comes to mind are the Korean War (1950-1953), and the impressive 1988 Summer Olympic Games in Seoul. But today Korea is emerging as a highly industrialized nation. From the ashes of the Korean War to the present, Korea has experienced a growing reputation as an economic miracle and an industrial "Superstar" of the 20th century. Consequently, much interest in Korea from the west has been stimulated in the last decade.

The celebration of the 1988 Summer Olympic Games held in Seoul, Korea opened the door to many visitors. It was a rare glimpse at the people and country of Korea as well as an opportunity for personal experiences of the Korean life style and traditional culture. Observers were struck by the beauty and the special forms of Korean costumes which are unique in Asia and the world. The image of this unique, elegant *hanbok* with its vibrant colors and exotic motifs relentlessly remained. This image was highlighted by the luxurious brocades used for the *juhgori* (jackets), *chima* (skirts), and *durumagi* (outer coats) in the winter, and the gossamer stiffened silk gauze *sa*, reminiscent of cicada's wings, for summer costumes. It was obvious that just as there were a myriad of fabrics their uses were just as varied and unique.

As a native Korean, I have happy childhood memories. I loved watching and helping my mother select fabrics from a visiting merchant who served our family home for years to make *hanbok* for the entire family for special occasions like New Year's Day, weddings, birthdays, and *Choosuhk* (Korean Thanksgiving day). My interest in Korean costume grew as I remembered how the grizzled merchant would describe in vivid detail the materials, colors, and textures he displayed. I remember the exhilarating feelings I had when all dressed up in a beautiful *hanbok*, our native dress. I became more curious about the costumes I saw around me. Who created the styles and from where had they originated? What meanings did the motifs and designs have? What significance did the different styles and the different fabrics have to Koreans in different places in society and in different times? What kinds of accessories were used with certain costumes? It became a personal goal and dream to produce a book that would answer these questions.

I began to have a growing desire to regain a sense of identity with my ancestors, and to provide and share some knowledge of Korea's great, rich, and fascinating heritage of 5000 years with my children, children of my friends, and people around the world. I became extremely interested in learning more about the unique, beautiful, and elegant *hanbok* for the better understanding of Korea's culture and tradition.

I searched for an introductory book in English, but I found that there were only a few and their coverage was meager. To satisfy my own curiosity, my children's and the westerner's, and in an attempt to provide a glimpse of what it may have been like in the past, I began to research and collect information about the history, motifs, and styles used for the emperor and the empress, the king and the queen, the *yangban* (nobility), Confucian scholars, Buddhist monks, and commoners during the 500 years of the Yi Dynasty (1392-1910).

This book is the result, a combination of relatively simple explanations and illustrative examples.

Hand-crafted arts, weaving, dyeing, sewing, and embroidering, are increasingly being replaced by mass-production. In Korea, there are a number of artisans and craftsmen demonstrating their indomitable spirit, by striving to maintain a dying tradition tenaciously using age-old methods, refining them and contributing to contemporary Korean life. In an attempt to show a glimpse into what may be possible in the future, I have included some of the alternate uses of Korean traditional fabrics, designs, and accessories devised by today's innovative artisans.

In the process of research, I had a wonderful opportunity to meet with all those who were talented, inspirational, and eager to provide the materials for this book. I sincerely appreciate their help. I am especially grateful to Cynthia Tennent Sohn for editing my manuscript with much understanding, patience, and many helpful suggestions; Shin Sook-won for valuable guidance, Ella Yang, my daughter, for her final editing, Park Kae-hee, Sung Ok-hi, and Limb Hijoo for their interests and encouragements, and support from Park Ae-kyoung. I wish to express my sincere appreciation to Sam Yuh, a graphic designer, for providing me invaluable artistic assistance. I'd like to thank Ham Ki-man and Han Joo-ri of Hollym for their help, and especially, to the late Rhimm Insoo for his enthusiasm.

Last, but not least, thanks to my husband Insuk, who was a valuable critic, counselor, and who made every effort to ensure this project's success.

Table of Contents

Foreword _ 6

Preface _ 8

Chronological Comparison Chart _ _ _ _ _ _ _ _ _ _ _ _ 13

Introduction _ 14

1   **Prehistoric Age (Paleolithic Age - 57 B.C.)** _ _ _ _ _ _ _ _ 17

2   **The Three Kingdoms Period** _ _ _ _ _ _ _ _ _ _ _ _ _ _ 21
     THE OLD SHILLA   (57 B.C. - 668 A.D.) _ _ _ _ _ _ _ _ _ _ _ _ _ _ _ 22
     THE KOGURYO   (37 B.C.- 668 A. D.) _ _ _ _ _ _ _ _ _ _ _ _ _ _ 26
     THE PAEKCHE   (18 B.C. - 660 A.D.) _ _ _ _ _ _ _ _ _ _ _ _ _ _ 33
     THE UNIFIED SHILLA (668 A.D. - 935 A.D.) _ _ _ _ _ _ _ _ _ _ _ _ _ 35

3   **The Koryo Kingdom (918 A.D. - 1392 A.D.)** _ _ _ _ _ _ 45

4 The Yi Dynasty (1392-1910) _____ 53
BASIC *HANBOK* _____ 56
OFFICIAL DRESS FOR MEN _____ 62
OFFICIAL DRESS FOR WOMEN _____ 96
DRESS OF THE COMMONERS _____ 126
DRESS FOR OTHER MEMBERS _____ 136
COSTUME FOR SPECIAL OCCASIONS _____ 152
THE END OF THE YI DYNASTY _____ 167

5 The Modernization Era (1800-1947) _____ 169
CHANGES OF MEN'S CLOTHING _____ 170
MEN'S HEADDRESS _____ 177
CHANGE OF WOMEN'S CLOTHING AND ACCESSORIES _____ 179
WOMEN'S HEADDRESS _____ 181

6 Contemporary Creations (1948-   ) _____ 183

Bibliography _____ 206

Sources _____ 208

Index _____ 210

Maps

Ancient Time

Three Kingdoms

Koryo

Yi Dynasty

Chronological Comparison Chart

	Korea	The West
B.C.	Paleolithic Age Neolithic Age	
5000	Tangun and founding of Korea (2333)	Early Mesopotamia Egyptian Kingdoms
2000 1000	Bronze Age Ancient Choson	Greek City-States Rome Founded (735)
500	Iron Age Puyo	Socrates (470 - 399) Alexander the Great (356 - 323) 1st Punic War (264 - 241) 2nd Punic War (219 - 201)
200	Confederated Kingdoms of Sam Han (Three Han States)	Julius Caesar (101 - 44)
100	Three Kingdoms: Old Shilla (57 BC - 668 AD) Koguryo (37 BC - 668 AD) Paekche (18 BC - 660 AD) Kaya (42 BC - 562 AD) Unified Shilla (668 AD -935)	Jesus born
A.D. 200 300		Christianity becomes state religion of Rome (392) Roman Empire split (395)
400		Anglo-Saxon established in Britain (449)
500		Mohammed (570-632)
600		Hegira (622) and Beginning of Islamic era
700 800		Charlemagne Crowned First Holy Roman Emperor (800)
900	Koryo Kingdom (918-1392)	
1000		First Crusade (1096-1099)
1100 1200		Magna Carta (1215) Marco Polo (1254-1324)
1300	Choson Kingdom (1392-1910) by Yi Family	Hundred Years' War (1334-1434)
1400		Columbus Voyages (1492-1504)
1500		Martin Luther Church Reform (1517)
1600		Thirty Years' War (1618-1648)
1700		American Revolution (1766) French Revolution (1789)
1800	Taehan Empire (1897-1910)	American Civil War (1861-1865)
1900	Annexation by Japan (1910) Establishment of Republic of Korea (1948)	World War I (1914-1918) World War II (1939-1945)

Introduction

Korea is one of the oldest countries in the world, having a 4300-year-old history. Although Korea is only about half the size of California, the population of South Korea today is more than 41 million. Korea, known in the west as "The Land of Morning Calm", is a rugged and beautiful country with four distinctive seasons. The southern parts of Korea are subtropical while the northern regions are arid and dry like Siberia. The summer is short, but hot and humid with a rainy period in June and July. The autumn is cool and crisp with clear, high, blue skies. This is the time rice paddies turn to a golden yellow, and maples and ginkgoes to rich, breathtakingly vibrant colors. Winter brings cold, dry air from Siberia with the temperature averaging little below 26°F (-3°C) in the south and 13°F (-11°C) in the north. But it is pleasant to see the snow covered up-turned traditional tile roofs and pine trees. Then suddenly the warm spring bursts open with the pink flowering azaleas and splashes of bright yellow forsythias all over the country. Waves of people in colorful Korean costumes flutter in the spring breeze, spilling out for picnics or flower viewing.

Korea is a peninsula stretching southward into the sea on the eastern end of the Asiatic land mass. It is surrounded by the Yellow Sea (Western Sea), East Sea, and South Sea. Across the South Sea lie the Japanese islands. The Yalu and Duman Rivers form the northern boundary with China's Manchuria and Russia's Maritime Province in the north, and Baektu Mountain in between runs to Halla Mountain on Cheju Island in the south. Notably, from ancient times to the 10th century, Korea's territory included a great part of Manchuria, the area east of the Liao River, and the Maritime Province of Russia.

This unique geographic position of being sandwiched between Russia, China, and Japan was the cause of frequent battles and brought about many unhappy events for Korea. Korea has been invaded by the Japanese, Chinese, and Russians often throughout the centuries, and once even lost her sovereignty and independence to an aggressor which is the bitterest experience Koreans ever had in their history. Koreans have had to suffer many hardships which continue into the 20th century. Unfortunately, today Korea is divided into north and south, and only about 20% of her land is arable. However Koreans have been able to preserve a great heritage and cultivate a unique cultural tradition, proving that they can endure hardships and continue to develop as an economic power in times of national crisis and catastrophe.

The costume of earlier periods is almost totally nonexistent because of its fragile nature (fabrics are subject to chemical change and deterioration), and also because clothes were not regarded as precious objects by Koreans whose frugal life style consisted of recycling garments until threadbare. Fortunately, there are literary records, paintings, relics and portraits depicting ceremonial costumes of the upper class. Knowledge of traditional Korean clothing is limited and more weighted towards the past two centuries.

Traditionally clothing has been and will continue to be important to human beings. Clothing plays a subtle yet important part of people's lives from birth to death, reflecting tastes, dreams, and histories. There is no better way to get to know another culture than by studying its costumes. Thus the traditional Korean costume provides us a glimpse of her past, representing hundreds of years of colorful history before the rush of modernization. The Korean costume reflects the cultural involvement of the aristocrats, nobility, and commoners in very distinct ways.

Koreans have always been close to nature. Shamanism, Taoism, Buddhism, and Confucianism all impacted the Korean's strong links with nature in all her familiar forms. This has been transferred into its art forms. Korean's keen appreciation and consciousness of the seasons, love of nature and sensitivity to color, symbolic motifs of Oriental myth and image, taste, value, and style, are carefully expressed in the details of *Hanbok*, Korean traditional costume. *Hanbok* worn by Korean men and women illustrate the good taste and quiet dignity of the country. To glimpse the elegant Korean costume is to discover much of the charm and fascination of its people and culture, and to better know the tradition and life style of the land once known as the "Hermit Kingdom". The Korean woman who has the serenity of Buddha, the mysterious calm of Taoism, and the ethical insight of Confucianism, is considered an unusually refined person. Wearing the carefully chosen *Hanbok* with its beautiful material, color, and motifs not only heightens the feeling of nature, but also is a grand celebration of life.

15

Note

The content is arranged in chronological order, abbreviations have been used for measurements, Korean terminology has been used wherever possible. For the name of the last dynasty (1392-1910 A.D.), Yi has been used instead of Choson, following the general usage by the Western historians not to be confused with the old Choson. Korean names are in traditional form, surname followed by given names.

The Romanization of Korean words, except widely known places and personal names, is used according to the closest sound with Korean alphabet. The following rule will make it easier to pronounce more accurately Korean words transliterated into English.

The vowels pronounced as follows:

아	*a* or *ah*	like the *a* in *father*	우	*u* or *oo*	like the *u* in *truth* or *wood*
야	*ya* or *yah*	like the *ya* in *yard*	유	*you* or *yoo*	like the *you* in *you*
어	*uh*	like the *uh* in *usher*	으	*eu*	like the *eu* in *en peu* in French
여	*yuh*	like the *yu* in *yuppie*	이	*ee* or i	like the *i* in *Indian*
오	*o* or *oh*	like the *o* in *Ohio*	애	*e* or *ae*	like the *e* in *egg*
요	*yo*	like the *yo* in *yoyo*	예,얘	*yae* or *ye*	like the *ye* in *yes*

Two vowels in a raw should be pronounced separately with a few exceptions. Thus, *ai* should be read *a i*. However, *ae* is like *a* in *egg* or *apple*.

The consonants are pronounced as follows:

ㄱ	*g*	like the *g* in *girl*	ㅇ	*ng*	like the *ng* in *gong*
ㄴ	*n*	like the *n* in *nation*	ㅈ	*j*	like the *j* in *John*
ㄷ	*d*	like the *d* in *day*	ㅊ	*ch* or *tch*	like *ch* or *tch* in *China*
ㄹ	*r* or *l*	like the *r* & *l* in *rain* & *lady*	ㅋ	*k*	like *k* in *kitchen*
ㅁ	*m*	like the *m* in *mother*	ㅌ	*t*	like *t* in *table*
ㅂ	*b*	like the *b* in *baby*	ㅍ	*p*	like *p* in *pay*
ㅅ	*s*	like the *s* in *sugar*	ㅎ	*h*	like *h* in *white*

Two consonants together (five exceptions) are pronounced as follows:

ㄲ	*g*	like *g* in *God*	ㅆ	*s*	like *s* in *Sam*
ㄸ	*d*	like *d* in *dam*	ㅉ	*j*	like *j* in *Jack*
ㅃ	*b*	like *b* in *bat*			

1

Prehistoric Age

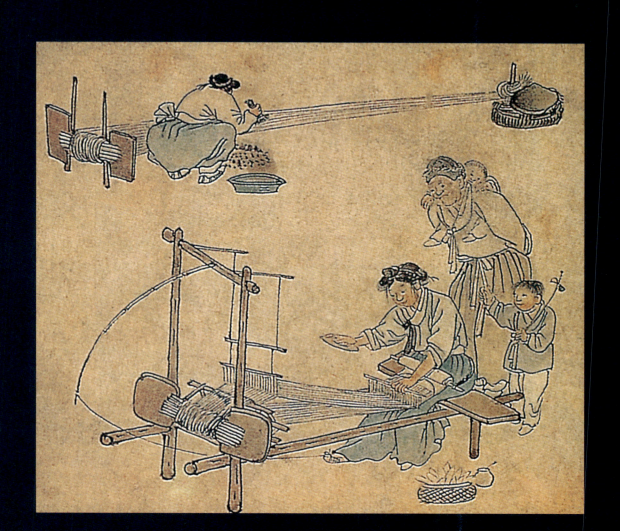

Prehistoric Age
(Paleolithic Age - 57 B.C.)

Although the early costume history of Korea is vague, archeologists have determined by archeological findings of hand-axes and chopper-scrapers that Paleolithic Age people lived in Korea about a half a million years ago. During the Neolithic Age, primitive nomads drifted into Manchuria and the northern part of the Korean peninsula, and lived by hunting and fishing and gathering fruits, edible roots, and berries. Protecting their bodies from the harmful elements of frigid winter cold and hot summer sun, human beings had begun to cover their bodies. Nudity had become shameful. Tree bark, vegetable fibers, leaves, and grass were used as fabric. In addition, animal and fish skins were used by scraping away the flesh with stone knives, then sewing them together using animal or fish bones as needles, and dried animal intestinal tissues or plant fibers as thread. Later, as the Neolithic people made spindles, they wove cloth and fishing nets.

The oldest costume-related materials discovered in Korea are Neolithic Age relics such as sewing needles, spinning and weaving spindles, and ornamental jade, earrings, and bracelets. Through these we can determine the origins of the costume of that period. Hand weaving has been a mainstay since the Neolithic Age. Hemp cloth was the first known fabric used for clothing and *myungju* (silk), until cotton seeds were brought back to Korea from China by a Korean envoy, Moon Ik-chom in 1363. Plant fibers were woven on primitive narrow back strap looms, by attaching a simple weaving device to one end of the weaver and to the other end a stationary object such as a tree. The later use of *mosi* (ramie), a fine fiber spun from an Asian perennial shrub plant, Boehmeria nivea of the nettle family, and strong, lustrous plant fiber, often resembled linen or silk. Varieties of silk for the more elegant wear of nobility brought a revolution in clothing. Although there is no clear evidence of the costume of this period, *Hangooksa-yuhnpyo* (Chronology of Korean History), *Buyojuhn* in *Samgookji* (Chinese History), and *Dong-eejuhn* in *Hoohansuh* (the Later Han Dynasty Record), described Korean tribal society;

> "· · · Puyo people [a northern tribe] revered white clothes and wore white *daemaepo* [jacket] and *baji* [trousers]· · · And Mahan (200 B.C.) people cultivated land for farming, cultivated hemp and mulberry trees to feed the cocoons with its leaves [knew sericulture] to make *myungju* (silk), wore *chohye* (straw sandals), wore necklaces and earrings, and men had their hair in *sangtu* (top-knot)".

This account confirms that as early as the Mahan period, animal furs and hemp fibers had been woven and fashioned into two-piece garments in Korea. Particularly in *Buyojuhn*, Puyo people wore dress made of silk, woven with patterns, silk without patterns, silk embroidered with threads of many colors, and fabric woven with animal furs (wool). They also wore straw sandals, and later, silk and leather shoes. Thus Korean costume evolved through the Bronze and the Iron Age. Completing the costume structure was *juhgori* (jacket), *chima* (skirt), *baji* (trouser) and *durumagi* (outer coat) as the base, with a hat, *ttwi* (belt), *hwa* (boots) or *ee* (shorter boots), and accessories like necklaces, bracelets, and rings. The defining characteristic of Korean costume was the use of different materials for fabric according to the four distinctively different seasons and the influence from the northern nomadic culture; that is narrow sleeves and trouser cuffs, under and outer garments all in a wrapping style due to the sub-arctic climate, and the tradition of having the opening in front like a caftan (the northern Mongol style). Later, at end of the Three Kingdoms period, the Tang Chinese style was adopted for royal families and nobility as formal wear, while Korean traditional clothes were worn as everyday wear. This created a dual clothing system for the upper class while the commoners only wore Korean traditional costumes.

Neolithic Age people lived in semi-subterranean pit-dwellings shaped like round or semi-rectangular dugouts with hearths at the center. Later as they moved down to rivers these pits had two hearths, and sometimes as many as five hearths. The *ondol* device of heating floors by channeling heat from kitchen fires through under-the-floor-flues developed from the hearths of these pit houses and is still used today.

It was natural for Korean people to sit on the *ondol* floors enjoying its warmth in the winter and coolness in the summer. It was natural that Korean costume also evolved according to the Korean life pattern of sitting on the floor. Traditionally Koreans removed their shoes at the door, sat on

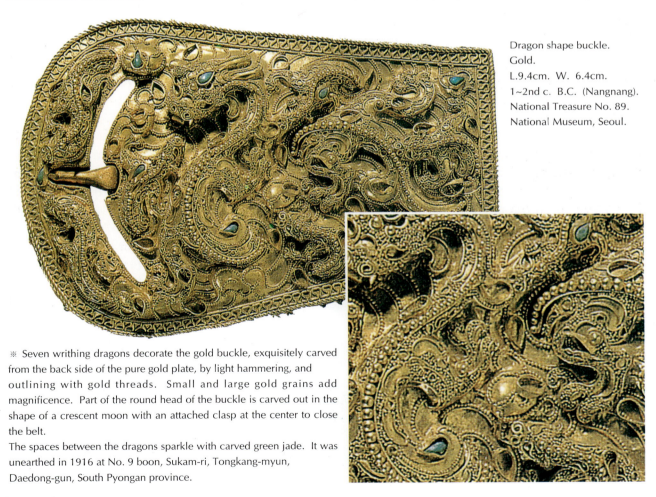

Dragon shape buckle.
Gold.
L.9.4cm. W. 6.4cm.
1~2nd c. B.C. (Nangnang).
National Treasure No. 89.
National Museum, Seoul.

※ Seven writhing dragons decorate the gold buckle, exquisitely carved from the back side of the pure gold plate, by light hammering, and outlining with gold threads. Small and large gold grains add magnificence. Part of the round head of the buckle is carved out in the shape of a crescent moon with an attached clasp at the center to close the belt.
The spaces between the dragons sparkle with carved green jade. It was unearthed in 1916 at No. 9 boon, Sukam-ri, Tongkang-myun, Daedong-gun, South Pyongan province.

bangsuhk (silk-cushions), slept on *yo* (mattresses) and *eebul* (coverlets which were unrolled at night, and rerolled in the morning). In addition, they ate meals at small, low tables (about 10" high), which were set before them on these spotless *ondol* floors. Over the years etiquette developed as to how men and women should sit on the floor. ※

> ※ The proper way of a woman's sitting position is one knee bent but up-positioned supported by the other bent knee in half-lotus position, keeping back straight, two hands lightly on the top of the up-positioned knee. Meanwhile, a man in voluminous pantaloon-like pants should sit in the lotus position. Since even today many Korean households combine western style rooms with *ondol-bang*, the traditional Korean style rooms, the proper sitting positions are required.

It was not until 1800 that the king used an *uh-chowa* (throne) with dragon heads elaborately carved on the arm rests, and a whole piece of tiger or leopard skin thrown over the back of the chair to indicate absolute authority. A foot-stool of the finest wood was set in front of the throne.

From the nomadic tribal Tungus community a single kingdom, Korea, was founded by the legendary Dangun who was said to have been born of a father of heavenly descent and a woman from a bear-totem tribe in 2333 B.C., and named *Choson* (Morning Calm). Its capital was in present day Pyongyang, and lasted 1,200 years.

Around the 15th century B.C., the Bronze Age, increased food production by use of bronze tools, contributed to a population growth which led to further migration. (Some of these people possibly migrated to Kyushu, Japan.) The mastery of bronze technology brought inter-tribal competition for the conquest of different clans, and led to a rise of larger tribal societies.

The art of metal-craft progressed through the Iron Age (500 B.C.), and Chinese culture began to extend into the Korean peninsula around 300 B.C., when the northern Chinese state of Yuan expanded to the north-western borders of Korea. Thus Chinese military colonies existed in Pyongan province under the Chinese Han dynasty (108 B.C. and 313 A.D.). Korea's Old Choson Dynasty fell when it was invaded and occupied by Emperor Wu of China's Han dynasty in 108 B.C.. By 200 B.C. the state of Okjuh and Tongye emerged in the northeast and east-central area. At the same time, the three Han tribes formed a federation; Mahan controlled the central and southern region, Jinhan the southeast, and Pyunhan in the south-central part along the southern coast. While the Mahan was struggling against the Chinese, the Jinhan and Pyunhan contended with Japanese invaders in the south. Meanwhile, there were also power struggles within the Han federation itself. As a result, Mahan was consolidated into the Kingdom of Paekche (18 B.C.) and Jinhan became the Kingdom of Shilla (57 B.C.). At this time, the Kingdom of Koguryo emerged (37 B.C.) in the southern part of Manchuria and the northern Korean peninsula. During the 1st century B.C. these Three Kingdoms dominated the peninsula, a domination which lasted for 7 centuries.

Remarkable bronze belt-buckles of the Bronze Age in the shape of animals were unearthed in 1918 at Oun-dong, Yongchon, North Kyongsang province.

The Three Kingdoms Period

2

The costume of the Three Kingdoms was developed based on the costume of the Prehistoric period, the Ancient Choson, with Pyongyang as its center, and Puyo, Yemaek, Koguryo, Yae, and Okjuh in the north, and Mahan, Pyunhan, Jinhan in the south, according to the *Samgook Sagi* and *Samgook Yusa*. *Samgook Sagi* (History of the three Kingdoms) was published in 1145 by Kim Pu-sik, a Confucian scholar, and *Samgook Yusa* (Memorabilia of the Three Kingdoms) by Il-yon, a Buddhist monk, was published in the 13th century.

During the 1st century B.C., the small states grouped themselves into three larger entities to reduce the danger of being attacked by other strong enemies. Thus, three prominent kingdoms were in command of the peninsula for seven centuries, and the recorded history of Korea began. During the Three Kingdoms and through the Unified Shilla period, society became more organized, the central government became more powerful, and economic conditions improved. Confucianism, Buddhism, and Taoism influenced Korean cultural development.

The Old Shilla Kingdom
(57 B.C. - 668 A.D.)

The Old Shilla Kingdom was established first among the Three Kingdoms by Jinhan in the south-east, her capital remaining in Kyongju for almost one thousand years. The six small tribal units of Pyunhan became the Kaya state, situated to the west of the Nakdong River, between Paekche and Shilla. It had close contact by sea with the Han dynasty colony of Lolang to the north, and

with Japan. But the Kaya was taken over by the larger more powerful States of the Shilla in 562 A.D.

The clothes of the Shilla Kingdom were similar to those of Koguryo and Paekche. The men wore both wide and roomy pants, *gwanggo*, and narrow pants, *goonggo*, and *juhgori*, and the women wore *chima* and *juhgori*. King Bopheung (514-539 A.D.) established a system of dress in the Shilla Kingdom. White clothes of rough hemp with black hoods for men, and long hemp *chima* and *juhgori* with unadorned, twisted hair for women, were the most common garment for the general populace. At least since the Three Kingdoms period, Koreans have worn a distinctive style of clothing, *Hanbok*.

Chinese influence in traditional Korean costume came with the adoption of the Tang Dynasty, China, male costume in 648 A.D. and female costume in 644 A.D. On the advice of the priest Jajang, who had returned from China in 649, Shilla Queen Jinduck (647-654 A.D.) introduced Chinese dress for the court and civil servants. The one-piece mandarin silk robe was adopted for ceremonial functions for the court, royal families, and officials. Official ranks were distinguished by different colors, lengths and styles of clothing, making a clear distinction between upper and lower class. However, for everyday wear, aristocrats and commoners alike wore *juhgori* and *chima* for women, and *juhgori* and *baji* for men. Both Shilla Queen Sunduhk (632-647 A.D.) and Queen Jinduck (647-654 A.D.) sent envoys to China, and received envoys from Emperor Taizong of Tang, China. When Queen Jinduck died in 654 A.D., the Tang Emperor Gaozong sent envoys with 300 bolts of silk to her funeral, according to *Samgook Sagi*.

Queen Jinduck, according to historical

record, embroidered *O-un-taepyung-song* (more than one hundred Chinese characters praising the achievement of King Kojong of Tang, China) by herself and sent this to Kojong. This is a reflection on the embroidery culture of the period. The aristocrats, as their culture flourished, took a great interest in clothing. The upper class wore silk costumes decorated lavishly with gold, jade and embroidery. Women of nobility decorated their hair with jewels, and noble men wore gold crowns and luxurious silk costumes. The treasures unearthed from Kyongju include delicate gold bracelets, comma-shaped jade jewelry, earrings, bronze ware, a girdle of 17 gold pendants with jade and other stones, and a unique, priceless, elaborately ornate, helmet-like, gold crown worn by one of the 56 kings or queens of the Shilla a thousand years ago. These ornaments demonstrate the fine taste, and superbly delicate and highly sophisticated craftsmanship of the people of Korea's golden age.

Geum-gwan : Gold Crown & gold accessories

Throughout history, gold has been considered precious, eminent, and sacred, symbolizing the sun, the king, God, and purity. The *geum-gwan* worn by king, queens and the upper class for ceremonies and rituals were jeweled, dazzling diadems and evidence of a highly refined mastery of goldsmithing during the Shilla Kingdom.

A magnificent and splendid gold crown (National Treasure No. 191), which was possibly used only for rituals or funeral purposes was discovered from the Gold Crown Tomb in 1921. The crown is made of cut, gold sheet with exquisite ornaments of spangles, pendants with circlets, and comma-shaped jade pieces attached to

The Gold Crown with gold spangles with comma-shaped jades
Gold and jade.
H. 27.5 cm. (longest pendant, 30.3cm.)
Shilla, (57 B.C. - 668 A.D.)
Hwangnam-daechong (Gold Crown Tomb),
North Mound, Kyongju, 1974.
National Treasure No. 191.
Kyongju National Museum.

the ends of the pendants by gold wires. It is embellished further with linear engravings and festoons in relief. The crown ornaments moves in a golden brilliance at the slightest movement.

Similar crowns have been found in the Lucky Phoenix Tomb, Gold Bell Tomb, and the Tomb of the Heavenly Horse. Along with the crown, other gold metal masterpieces were developed in dazzling accessories such as necklaces, earrings, bracelets, and rings. This characterized the costume of the Three Kingdoms and brought its brilliant culture to its culmination.

As the Three Kingdoms were actively promoting intercultural exchanges with China, they helped the Japanese to lay cultural foundations. The Paekche made enormous contributions for the development of a new culture in Japan by exporting Confucianism and Buddhism. The Paekche sent Confucian scholars such as Achiki and Wang In, Buddhist monks and skilled workers, and introduced book learning in the 6th century. In the following century, medical doctors, historians, artists and technicians of Paekche were sent to Japan as well. A Koguryo monk, Hyeja, was Prince Shotoku's teacher, and a monk and painter, Damjing, taught Buddhism and art. The famous mural painting of the Horyu-ji (temple), near Nara, is a copy of Damjing's painting style. The Japanese learned the arts of painting, music, philosophy, agriculture and sewing from Korea, as well as religion.

According to the Japanese Embroidery Chronology No. 2, the Shilla sent its

Pair of earrings.
Gold.
L. 8.7cm.
Shilla (c. 5-7th A.D.).
Excavated from Bubu-chong (tomb of) Kyongju.
National Treasure No. 90.
National Museum, Seoul

The most splendid gold earrings of the Shilla had thick, hollow main rings, embellished with gold granules in a pattern of hexagons enclosing tiny circles. These were all crafted by attaching tiny grains of gold to the surface.
Another middle oval ring hung from the main ring, to which a pendant of two spherical elements hung, one below the other, and formed of small gold rings. Small, leaf-shape spangles, which were serrated at the edges and mid-rib to imitate granulation, were attached and fluttered with even the slightest vibration.
The lowest part was a seed-shaped drop which was elegantly designed and decorated with granulation. All of this was symbolic of the wearer's wealth, honor, and glory.

Bracelet with curled edges and jade inlay.
Gold.
Shilla (c. 507th A.D.).
Excavated from Hwangnam-daechong, Kyongju.
Kyongju Museum

Dae (girdle) with 17 pendants.
Gold and jade.
L. 120.0 cm. (longest pendant 77.5cm).
Shilla (c 5th-7th A.D.)
Hwangnam-daechong (North Mound, Kyongju,1974)
National Treasure No. 192.
Kyongju National Museum

Painting of a heavenly horse on a birch bark mudguard (saddle) surrounded by floral design in Chuhnma-chong.
Shilla.

embroidery techniques to Japan in 430 A.D. The *Chunsookukmandalla* wall hanging embroidered on silk is done by Ka Suh-ik, a Koguryo man, with some help from others, and was designated as a Japanese National Treasure and preserved in *Choong-goong-sa* in Japan. It shows costumes exactly the same as the costumes worn by people in the mural paintings of ancient Koguryo tombs. The Shilla also sent the technique of quilting to Japan, and it became a very famous quilting method called 'Shilla Quilting'.

25

Shin (shoes) of the Shilla were in the same design as Koguryo's *hwa* (mid-calf length boots) and *ee* (low sided shoes). The shoes excavated from an ancient tomb, the Shik-ri-chong, shows introduction of metal among materials used at that time, e.g. grass, cloth, and plant, to make *ee* shoes. In Shilla, *hwa* was worn mostly by men, and *ee* was more popular among women.

Buhsuhn (cotton socks), a typical Korean style sock of mid-calf length and up-turned pointed toes, was developed from the Three Kingdoms period. It had an elaborate sash decoration at the ankle, unlike the sash on a baby's *buhsuhn* of today which is for the practical purpose of keeping the *buhsuhn* in place. In this period the *buhsuhn* was made of a material similar to rough *ma* (hemp), not like today's *buhsuhn* which is made of fine cotton.

Buhsuhn (cotton socks)

Compared to Koguryo and Paekche, the Shilla created gold *dae* (girdle) with more elaborate ornaments, such as the gold *dae* from the Gold Crown Tomb (National Treasure No. 88), the Hwangnam-daechong (North Mound, National Treasure No. 192), Gold Bell Tomb, the Lucky Phoenix Tomb and the Tomb of the Heavenly Horse.

The Shilla upper class highly valued, and therefore encouraged, the development of paintings, architecture (Buddhist temples, royal tombs), literature (poems, historical records), metallurgy, science (oldest astronomical observation tower in the world), sculpture (Buddha's statues), and handicrafts and paintings associated with Buddhism.

The Koguryo Kingdom
(37 B.C.- 668 A.D.)

The Kingdom of Koguryo, the largest of the Three Kingdoms, was established in the northern part of the Korean peninsula and southern part of Manchuria, with its capital at Guknaesong (now Tung-gu) in the middle of the Yalu River region. As nomadic tribes its people came from the north, present-day Siberia and Manchuria, and brought Bronze culture to Korea. Koguryo was influenced by north-eastern China and the presence of a

Mural painting of Hunting Scene (*Suryupdo*) of 16th c. in Muyong-chong (tomb) in Guknaesong. Hunters on horse back wearing narrow-cuffed, short sleeved jackets and *juhlpoong* (hats with plumes).
Koguryo.

Chinese colony at Lolang from 108 B.C. to 313 A.D. By overthrowing the Lolang in 313, Chinese domination was removed completely from Korea, and its territory was expanded.

During the reign of King Gwanggaeto (391-414 A.D.) and his son, King Jangsu (413-91 A.D.), Koguryo's territory expanded to a great part of Manchuria. The Capital was moved to present day Pyongyang in 427 A.D. At this time contact was made with Chinese civilization by way of a land route. During Koguryo, Chinese characters were used for writing historical records, and a Confucian school was established in 372 A.D. to teach Confucian texts. According to the *Samgook Sagi*, Chinese classics were to remain the basis of Korean education until the 19th century. Koguryo was the first area of Korea to introduce Buddhism from China in 372 A.D. Buddhist influence is evident in mural paintings in tombs, the most impressive remains of Koguryo culture, fourteen of which are located near Guknaesong (Tung-gu), and thirty seven near Pyongyang. The mural paintings depict Koguryo people wearing a two-piece garment belted at the waist.

As the Three Kingdoms were firmly established with strong leaders, the class society developed into a pyramid shape. The kings, queens, and the aristocrats controlled the commoners. As they secured positions and wealth, they wanted to display their status through a dress code. The clothing they wore was determined by a strict system of class distinctions. Thus, the formless coverings of the prehistoric age were transformed into distinctive styles of costumes embellished with gold, silver, and embroideries to differentiate the rulers from the ruled, and the rich from the poor.

Two men in white *juhgori* which closed at the right side, and wearing black chaek (cap).
Tomb mural painting in Soosan-ri.
Koguryo (c. 5th B.C)

Mural painting of *Jangsado* in Samsil chong
Masculine man (*jangsa*) in *jambang-ee* and short sleeve jacket, wearing top-knot.(*sangtu*)
Koguryo

Although no evidence remains of clothing from this period, mural paintings in the Muyong-chong tomb of Koguryo in Tung-gu, Manchuria (4th-5th century) depict the costume of the Three Kingdoms period. Distinctive differences in the shapes and designs of men's and women's wear had become evident by this time.

During the Three Kingdoms period a separate *juhgori* (jacket), was worn by men and women of all ages and class. The hip-length men's *juhgori* had tube-like, wide and long sleeves, and closed at the left side with different colored bindings attached around the neckline, sleeve cuffs, hem line, and front opening. Through the years the method of closing the jacket has changed. First, the front opening of the *juhgori* closed at the front center in a caftan style, then the closing changed to the left side, and finally it changed to the right side which has been permanently accepted since the 6th c. A.D. Details of a mural painting in a Koguryo tomb (5th c.) in Soosan-ri show two men dressed in white hip-length jackets closed at the right side, and wearing black *chaek* (caps). To keep the jacket closed in place, a

Muyong-chong mural painting.
Men, women and boy servant at center, shows basic costume of the Three Kingdoms.
Koguryo (c. 5th B.C.).

ttwi (sash, belt, or cord) was used to fasten at the waist.

Similarly, women's *juhgori* had been worn in many ways, long or short, or with long and wide or short and narrow sleeves. The *juhgori* with red binding worn by a woman in the mural painting in Gakjuh-chong Tomb No. 3 in Anak, was waist-length (shorter than men's), short and narrow sleeved, and closed at the left front. This indicates that both long and short *juhgoris* were worn during the Three Kingdoms period. Although the practice of fastening jackets with *ttwi* was seen in Koguryo mural paintings, as the jacket length got shorter from the Koryo (935-1392) and the Yi (Choson, 1392-1910), the jacket was fastened with *goreum* (doubled and sewed up ribbons), and tied at the right side of the wearer's chest. This method of fastening the *juhgori* and *durumagi* (long outer coat) added interest to the simple style of traditional Korean everyday wear.

The *baji* (trouser) of Koguryo varied in style. Men wore *holtae* (skin tight pants), *goonggo* (narrow, straight legged, shorter trousers), *gwanggo* or *daegoogo* (roomy, wide-crotched, long pants) or *jambang-ee* (unlined

Woman in a black *juhgori* with red binding, which closed at the left side, and wearing *guhngwik* (head scarf).
Gakjuh-chong mural painting.
Koguryo (c. 5th B.C.).

shorts, knickers). The *baji* shown on the mural paintings of Koguryo tombs were worn by men and women as the bottom part of basic attire, worn under the outer garment or under the skirt. High ranking men wore *daegoogo* in different colors, and lower class men wore *goonggo* as work clothes just like *jambang-ee*, as shown on the mural painting of *Jangsado* (masculine man) in a Koguryo tomb in Samsil-chong.

Baji was a necessary part of the Korean costume even before the Three Kingdoms period. It provided better mobility for the horseback riding northern nomadic people.

The *chima* (skirts) were worn by both men and women as shown in Koguryo mural paintings in the tombs. There were two kinds of *chima*; *sang*, worn by both men and women for formal occasions, and long and wide *goon*, worn only by women. As shown in the mural painting of a Koguryo tomb in Ssangyong-chong, the three women's *chima*s are long and wide with narrow pleats all the way down to the hem line. The name for the skirt became *chima* permanently during the Yi Dynasty, and unlike *juhgori*, *chima* has changed very little since the Three Kingdoms period.

The *durumagi* was originally worn by northern Chinese people as cold-weather gear from ancient times. The long outer coats fell to mid-calf with bindings similar to the *juhgori* (sometimes double bindings). Later, the upper class adopted various forms of Chinese long outer coats for ceremonies and rituals, and eventually for daily use in a modified form called *durumagi* for people of all class, age, and sex, as an outer coat.

Samgookji, in *Buyojuhn*, describes Korean people wearing *durumagi* with wide sleeves, "…*Paek-po-dae-mae-po*". According to the mural painting in Koguryo tombs, there were two kinds of *durumagi*; wide and long sleeved and narrow and short sleeved, both with bindings for the neckline, front opening line and sleeve cuffs. *Durumagi* of

Ssangyong-chong mural painting.
Three women in long, pleated, full skirts, and hip-length jackets.
Koguryo (5th B.C.)

Muyong-chong mural painting (in Tung-gu, Manchuria).
Two ladies-in-waiting (or women servants) in *durumagi* (long coat) and *ttwi* tied at one side with baji under skirt, offering food to Buddha, the Four Cardinal Deities.
Koguryo (37 B.C. - A.D. 668).

※ *Durumagi* (long coat) and *juhgori* closed in front, *goreum* (doubled ribbon) tied at side for *durumagi*, and at the center for *juhgori*, to avoid piling up one goreum on the another in case *durumagi* and *juhgori* were worn at the same time.

Muyong-chong mural painting
Dancers, two women in pleated *chima* and *durumagi, baji* under the *chima*, and three men in hip length *juhgori* and *baji*.
Tomb of Dancers in Guknaesong (Tung-gu).
Koguryo (5th c.).

the Three Kingdoms period in mural paintings in Koguryo tombs and in *Paekche-gooksado* and *Samgook Sasindo*, are similar in form. *Durumagi* worn by the upper and lower classes during the Three Kingdoms was not only for cold weather but for ceremonies and rituals as formal attire.

In the mural painting of the Koguryo tomb, Gamshin-chong (4th-5th century), there are some traces of embroidery done in *dangcho muni* (scrolling-vine motifs) and a *wang-ja muni* (Chinese ideograph of a king) in silk clothes. According to the Chinese *Sasuh* (History book),

> "... Koguryo people wore silk hats and ceremonial dress of *geum* (patterned silk) and *soo* (embroidered silk). Another Chinese history book, Samgookji, in *Wuiji Koryo-juhn*, described how "Koguryo court ladies wore silk dress with embroidery for official occasions".

Hair Styles and Headdress

Hair styles of this period varied. The *jok* (chignon) hair style was braided hair, tied with *daenggi* (doubled ribbons), coiled, and finally pinned through the chignon with a *binyuh* (crossbar) at the nape of the neck. Sometimes for married women hair was braided, piled-up, and arranged on the top of the head.

An example of hair arranged on the top of the head is seen in the mural portrait of Queen Michun in Koguryo tomb No. 3 in Anak, one of more than 50 chambered tombs scattered in the Tung-gu plain across the Amnok River in Manchuria and in the vicinity of Pyongyang (Koguryo's capital). This tomb is known to have been built in the year 357 A.D. and depicts the customs of the period.

Traditionally, unmarried men continued to have a ponytail or single braided queues (plaits) down their backs which were tied with strings. For unmarried men and women, tying hair with a black or red *daenggi* (wide doubled ribbon), instead of string, was revived by the Yuan, China influence at end of Koryo period. *Sangtu*

❶ Men wearing *gaht* in genre painting. Yi Dynasty

❷ Two men wearing *chaek*. Mural painting in Susan-ri tomb. Koguryo

❸ The mural of Tomb No. 3 in Anak Queen Michun and ladies-in-waiting with hair arranged on top of the head. Koguryo (357 A.D.).

(top-knot) and double *sangtu* hair styles for married men became permanent during this period. Under the *gaht* (hat made of horse hair) a small black rimless horsehair beanie actually covered the top-knot. Around the forehead a horse hair headband, *mangguhn*, was worn to secure the *gaht* on the head.

Thus, in an ancient mural of the Koguryo tombs, men's *sangtu* look much larger than the *sangtu* worn during the Yi Dynasty.

Head gear of some kind was worn from the Neolithic Age to the Three Kingdoms period as protection from cold weather and shade from the sun. The *Samgookji* (Chinese

Gaht worn by men. / Mural painting in Gamshin-chong. Koguryo

History), *Buyojuhn*, records reveal "Puyo people wore hats decorated with gold and silver". During the Three Kingdoms period, people wore these hats made of silk, bark of white birch, leather, and horse hair. Women wore a *guhn*. The *guhn* or *guhngwik* (a folded cloth scarf forming a triangle at the top) can be seen in the mural painting of Gakjuh-chong, where a woman wearing black *juhgori* with a red binding closing on the left side, is wearing a *guhngwik*. The *julpoong-mo* was a hat made of the bark of white birch with a triangular pointed top, and decorated with gold and silver. Koguryo people inserted plumes in the *julpoong-mo*. The *chaek*, a hat with more than three divisions in back, a low front, and high pointed back, was worn mostly by officials, according to the *Samgookji*, in *Wuiji dong-eejuhn*. The *chaek* can be seen in the mural painting of Koguryo King Michun (Tomb No. 2, No. 3, in Anak, Yaksu-ri and Susan-ri). The *gaht*, worn by a hunter in a Koguryo tomb mural painting in Gamshin-chong, is very close to a later style. The Sui Shu records reveal that the Koguryo aristocracy wore purple silk caps with gold and silver ornaments, and others wore caps with bird's wing ornaments.

It is obvious that besides the fabulous and unique costumes of Korea the variety of head gear alone was simply marvelous.

Gold crowns were worn by kings and queens and high ranking officials for ceremonies and rituals during this period. The oldest and most unique Korean *geumgwan* (gold crown) in the less elaborate style can be seen in the mural paintings in the Koguryo tombs.

From these basic crowns evolved the most impressive and unique gold crowns of the Shilla Kingdom, which are unparalleled. These highly refined gold crowns were worn by the upper class in all Three Kingdoms, in Kaya and Shilla in particular. Along with the gold crown, gold accessories such as necklaces, earrings, bracelets, and rings, were developed creating a glorious gold accessory culture. These gold accessories became characteristic of the Three Kingdoms costume culture, and led the splendid art of goldsmithing to its zenith.

Early forms of shoes made of straw, plants, cloth and leather were worn by people before the Three Kingdoms period, according to *Samgookji* (the Chinese History). Therefore shoes developed from the Three Kingdoms period based on these primitive shoes.

Shin (shoes) in Koguryo were either *ee* (ankle length) or *hwa* (mid-calf length thick soled boots). According to documented record, there were *juhkpihwa* (red leather mid-calf length) and *opihwa* (thin leather). The *hwa* is shown in the mural painting in Ssangyong-chong, while the *baeksaekhwa* (white leather mid-calf length) is shown in the mural painting of 'Hunting Scene' in Muyong-chong.

Dae (belts or girdles), an excavated relic of the Bronze period, must have been used by the tribal people in the Bronze Age. By the Three Kingdoms period *dae* were used not only as a simple, practical medium to keep the jacket closed, but also to distinguish ranks as well as ornament. Koguryo nobility wore wide *dae* made of either silk or fine hemp, while commoners wore narrower *dae*, and the lower classes wore cords of twisted threads.

The custom of wearing *dae* with small ornaments seems to have originated in the northern nomadic tradition, and probably came to Shilla from China via Paekche (origins in Han dynasty or earlier). Tomb engravings of the Tang dynasty show attendants wearing narrow leather belts with hanging pendants of varying lengths. The elegantly refined Korean *dae* of the Three Kingdoms continued until the early part of Koryo.

After the fall of Koguryo in 668 the tradition of mural painting in tombs was no longer continued in Korea, but it had already been transmitted to Japan. A good example is the Takamatsu-zuka tomb which shows the influence of Koguryo style and subject matter.

The Paekche Kingdom
(18 B.C. - 660 A.D.)

The Kingdom of Paekche, a tribal unit of the Mahan, was located in the south-west region of the Korean peninsula with her capital city in present day Seoul and territory encompassing the Hwanghae, Kyonggi, North and South Chungchong and Cholla provinces. King Muryong's effort to stand against the Koguryo's threats had failed, and Koguryo pushed her capital to Ungjin (now Kongju) first and then to Sabi (now Puyo) in

538. Paekche relied on sea routes, and had good political and cultural relations with southern China and Japan. For geographical reasons, the spread of Chinese influence to Paekche took a longer time than Koguryo. But Paekche was already sending her culture to Japan. According to the *Samgook Sagi's* description of Paekche custom, "···on a propitious day in May, Paekche people wore wide sleeved, reddish-purple tops, blue trousers, and hats with flowers and birds embroidered in gold, and wore leather girdles and shoes for official functions". It indicated that the embroidery culture of Paekche was as advanced as Koguryo. Notably, the Paekche King Goi in 285 A.D. sent a Paekche woman weaver, Suh So, to Japan to teach weaving, dying and clothes making, according to *Hangooksa-yuhnpyo* (Chronology of Korean History). A system of official uniforms was established by King Goi in 260 A.D. In 384, a Chinese monk came to Paekche and built the first Buddhist temple in 385. Consequently, Buddhism became the state religion.

Paekche men also wore *baji* and *juhgori*, and women, *chima* and *juhgori*, which was similar to Koguryo. But the *baji* worn by Paekche leaders were wide and roomy with bindings attached at the cuffs that did not tie with *daenim* (small sashes) around the ankles. The costumes of the rulers were elaborate and colorful, and those of the ruled were basic and made from humble materials, like hemp, in white or earthy colors.

The clothes of commoner women were long and wide sleeved with jackets which tied in the front. The hair of married women was braided into two pigtails, twisted, and arranged on the top of head. Unmarried women had pigtails which hung down their backs.

Shin (shoes) of the Paekche Kings were *o-hyuk-ee* (thin leather and ankle length). The metal shoes excavated from the Tomb of Paekche King Muryong had 9 spikes (c. 6th c.). Although it is not clear, the commoners and the lower class must have worn distinctively different kinds of shoes.

Paekche differentiated ranks by *dae* of different colors for the upper class, while the lower class wore *dae* of humble kinds.

The Paekche's advanced architectural skills and interior designs were found in the Tomb of King Muryong near Kongju and Puyo. (Again, there is evidence that these skills were passed on to Japan. In Nara, Japan, a wood sculpture, the Kudara Kwanon, was made from a single wood block by Paekche artists living in Japan.) The tomb of King Muryong, the last ruler of Paekche, was discovered in Kongju in 1971 by a laborer working on the drainage behind the tomb who accidentally struck a brick which turned out to be the part of the tomb of King Muryong. The tomb was found completely undisturbed since it was sealed in the early 6th century. According to Liang Dynasty China history, Paekche Kings wore a black silk diadem (crown) with gold floral ornaments attached in the front and back. A pair of such ornaments was found in the tomb near the king's head pillow.

There were valuable and exquisite tiny beads, gold earrings, and a girdle with a long, silver pendant. Two bronze mirrors, a queen's gold necklace, gold and silver bracelets, gold earrings, and two gold crowns, of extremely fine craftsmanship, in the shape of flowers and flames, were also found. Of course, all the organic materials in the coffin had disappeared. But gold, silver, and glass objects remained intact.

The King's crown is larger than the Queen's in size and more ornate with exquisite flower designs. The style of Paekche crowns were different from the crowns of the Shilla period. While the Shilla crown was characterized by straight lines and sharp angles, the Paekche crown was adorned by curvaceous, flowing lines.

Compared to the ornate and exquisite Gold crowns and earrings, the necklace is very simple, without decoration, reminiscent of contemporary necklaces.

Metal shoes, *geum-dong-ee* with 9 spikes excavated from the tomb of Paekche King Muryong Paekche.
Kongju National Museum.
Kongju, Cholla Province

Dwitkkoji (ornamental three pronged hairpin worn on back).
Gold. / L. 18.4cm.
Paekche (523 A.D.)
Excavated from the Tomb of the King Muryong in 1971.
National Treasure No. 159.
Kongju National Museum

The Unified Shilla
(668 - 935 A.D.)

With the help of Tang China, Shilla took over its rivals, the Kingdoms of Koguryo and Paekche, unifying the whole peninsula (668 A.D. - 935 A.D.), and laying the foundations for the homogeneous culture and society that has continued from Koryo until the present day.

Because of open sea routes, the Unified Shilla Kingdom was able to exchange ideas and skills with the Tang Empire of Dynasty China. From this exchange, during the Three Kingdoms period, clothing from China was introduced. Korea enjoyed peace without domestic conflict and foreign invasion, and grew very prosperous. For over two and a half centuries, in an era which was to be known as Korea's "Golden Age", the Unified Great Shilla reached a zenith.

Korean figurines unearthed from a mid-8th century tomb in Kyongju, the capital city of the Shilla Kingdom, wore Chinese-style dress. In other earlier tomb mural paintings, long jackets with belts at the waist were worn over pleated, long skirts. But Unified Shilla period figurines wore skirts over their jackets, a distinctively Tang Chinese style.

The Unified Shilla people indulged in wealth, luxuries, and splendor, and lived easy, idle lives to the extreme. In the year

Comb (lady's), Hawksbill. Unified Shilla (668 - 935 A.D.)

※ The fine-toothed ornamental lady's combs were made of hawksbill (turtle shell) decorated with flower-leaf motifs in gold and sapphire inlay, and *dwitkkoji* (hairpins) tops in the shape of Gingko leaves with three prongs for the hair at the back which would complement the flame-like ornament of kings' and queens' head-dress.

834, Shilla King Hongdok decreed sumptuary laws repeatedly against the upper class's extravagance in every aspect of their lives, expensive fabrics, embroidered silks, and embroidered silk folding screens, in particular. Prosperity, cultural development, and trade with China improved living standards, and the upper class demanded more elaborate clothing, leading to even more ornate clothing in spite of the sumptuary laws decreed by King Hongdok. The aristocrats continued to live extravagantly, failing to notice social chaos and the declining morale of the people. This created a heavy burden on the commoners. The influence and strength of the government soon deteriorated and lost the vitality that brought it to power, causing it to neglect the welfare of the people. Finally in 935 A.D., the last king of Shilla surrendered to Koryo, which was founded by one rebel leader, General Wang Kon, ending 100 years of unity and peace of the Shilla Kingdom. And a new dynasty, the Kingdom of Koryo was founded (918-1392).

● **Fabrics during the Three Kingdoms Period**

The main method of weaving in Korea has been flat weave, twill weave, satin weave, gauze weave, and tapestry weave, all of these being universal techniques. Satin weave is one of the basic weave structures in which filling threads are interlaced with the warp at widely separated intervals, producing the effect of an unbroken surface (plain weave or twill weave). Luxurious fabrics are woven by the satin weave. Each weft thread floats over many warp threads, creating a smooth, shiny surface. Twill weave basically relies on the reflected light to reveal its patterns, which are woven by passing a weft thread over or under two or more warp threads. The pattern can be woven on a plain or twill background, or it can be reversed with a twilled pattern on a twilled background going in the same or opposite direction as that of the pattern.

During Shilla King Yurinisaryong's (ninth year of reign), this court arranged a weaving contest among two groups of noble ladies, with the princess as judge. The winners were served a fine meal prepared by the losers as reward, after which they all sang and danced.

During this periods, dye was rare and available only to the upper class, and the variety of dye was also limited. Certain dyes,

Women in weaving process. / Genre painting by Ki-san. / 19th c.

such as red, purple, and yellow were not allowed for use by commoners, resulting in the white clothed populace. But later, vegetables, plants, roots, flowers, berries, mineral and other kinds of natural dyes were widely used in Korea.

Sambae : Hemp

A hemp plant is an annual which has straight stems topped by leaves, and is about 2 to 2.5 meter tall. Descending from a wild plant that grew throughout Central Asia, the botanical name of the plant is 'Cannabis sativa'. The seeds were planted at the end of the 3rd month of the lunar calendar. Yellow

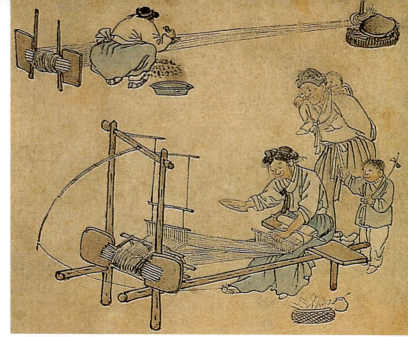

Women weaving hemp.
Genre painting by Tanwon (Kim Hong-do).
18th c.

flowers bloomed in the 7th and 8th month, and the plants were cut only once a year after the 11th month. *Sambae* (or *ma-po*), hemp cloth, a strong, durable, canvas-like textile was made from the fibers of the hemp plant by stripping the bark from the stems of the plant. Hemp cloth from northern Korea, Hamkyoung province, were considered superior and called *puk-po*. In the south, hemp cloth was produced mostly in Kyongsang province and called *young-po*. The most excellent hemp cloth was produced in Andong, North Kyongsang province in the south, known as *andong-po*.

The hemp from Kangwon province was not as superior and was used for general clothing for farmers and for funeral rites, and called *gang-po*, according to *Ko Sa Tong* (Ancient History Document).

Hemp flourished in poor soil and extreme weather conditions. The fibers were obtained from the center of the stalks under the outer bark and these fibers were separated from the woody parts of the plant by retting and boiling, as with flax for linen, then by subjecting them to moisture and bacteria. They were soaked in water for twelve to twenty-four hours and then covered with matting to ferment. A common way of making them into a yarn was to tie or connect the small fibers end to end by twisting or gluing them with saliva. Hemp fibers are thicker than ramie, but fine ones are almost as thin as mid grade ramie.

Each stage of the labor-intensive and time-consuming process, from the twisting of the fibers to the weaving of the threads into fabric, was mostly done by women. The weaving technique of using primitive back-strap looms has not changed up to the present. This weaving technique is also used to make *mosi* (ramie).

Mosi : Ramie

Mosi (ramie), a fine spun fiber, is obtained from the shrub 'Boehmeria nivea', a perennial which grows up to 2 meters and multiplies by roots (and cuttings). Its leaves are wide and have serrated edges.

There are male and female flowers on the same tree which bloom in between the summer and fall. The stalks are cut in the same year of planting or the next year when the base of the stem color changes to brown and the leaves begin to dry. The best and most famous ramie, *Hansan Mosi*, still comes from Hansan, South Chungchong province, while the weaving technique has been handed down from mother to daughter.

Hansan Mosi was very thin, even, strong, and always looked new even after many washes. *Mosi* was considered a very precious and costly commodity. Thus, even small scraps were to make into mats and string to used as lining for young rice plants.

Hansan mosi was designated as an Important Intangible Cultural Asset in 1966, and *Sambae* was designated as an Important Intangible Cultural Asset No. 32 in 1970.

Saeng mosi (natural ramie) man's jacket

Chima, juhgori & *durumagi* made of light green colored *mosi* by Park Sun-young

Woman in white *mosi hanbok* & *norigae* by Park Sun-young

***Sa* and *Ra* : Stiffened silk gauze**

Light weight summer silks are mostly of the *sa* variety, and of openwork weave similar to gauze. Loose, open mesh, simple weave, *sa*, is followed by *ra* which is distinguished by strips of densely woven material separated by an open weave. These transparent silks were developed in ancient times. Gauze originated in Palestine and spread to the west and east, arriving in China as early as 200 B.C. It soon moved on to Korea. The secret of these open weave fabrics was the twisting of their fine warp threads into pairs.

Weft threads were inserted between the twists, forming an open weave that was strong, beautiful, and cool. They were like gossamer, nearly transparent, and in many cases were called *hwamunsa* (flower patterned *sa*), *unmunsa* (cloud), or *yongmun-sa* (dragon), and so on. Also they were distinguished by their texture into softer *sookgosa* (prepared or processed) and stiffer *saenggosa* (raw). The best quality of *sa* was called *gap-sa*. Closely related to *sa* was another type called *hang-ra* which was also almost transparent and had parallel lines created by skipping the weft at intervals. However, *hang-ra* was not always made of silk, and could be a very fine ramie or cotton which was very suitable for making summer wear. Motifs of small summer flowers, grasses, insects, small Chinese characters for good fortune, long life, or happiness, were woven, embroidered, or hand painted on the fabric.

Dang-ui (Minor ceremonial jacket)
Green *Saenggosa* with Chinese character for longevity and gourd motif.
L. 83.5 cm. / W. of sleeves. 68 cm. / 1890s.
Ewha Womans Univ. Museum, Seoul.

Myungju : Soft silk 'pongee'

Myungju also has a long history in Korea. It is believed that sericulture was practiced for silk before 200 B.C. by the Mahan people, and mulberry trees had been planted throughout Korea.

The soft, silky, lustrous threads were obtained as a filament from the cocoon of the caterpillars or moth called silkworms. The silkworm larva (the immature wingless, feeding stage of an insect that undergoes complete metamorphosis), of the Chinese silkworm moth, Bombyx mori, pushes out silk strands from its lower lip to form a cocoon. The soft silk threads were formed by placing cocoons into boiling water. When these cocoons were softened sufficiently, the end of the fine fiber was found and gradually the silk was pulled from the cocoon by a spinning wheel into long filaments by silk-workers. The filaments were strengthened and colored for use in weaving, embroidery, and sewing. This light-weight soft silk (*myungju*) was thin but not transparent, and was warm enough to be used for winter wear.

Dyed natural *myungju* fabric

Saeng-myungju chima & *juhgori* for summer by Park Sun-young
1990s

Women working in sericulture in Korean costume.
Genre painting. / 19th c.

※ In the painting, women wore layers of underwear to make volume of the skirt; shows color combinations of jacket and skirt; younger women have chignons and elderly woman have piled-up hair style and wore all white clothes, while unmarried women have braided hair and wore yellow *samhoejang* jacket and red skirt.

Close up of *yang-dan*

Dan : Opaque silk

Opaque silks of relatively heavy weight are called *dan*. There are two main varieties of *dan*; *gong-dan* (satin) and *mobon-dan* (damask), which are almost of the same thickness. A slightly heavier variety called *yang-dan* can be patterned in the same color, or in two or more colors. Therefore, *yang-dan* is translated generally as brocade. This type of satin weave employed colored, floating threads, which lay on top of the fabric much like embroidery. To weave these rainbow colors into the fabric, the threads were wound on small bobbins. Attached at both ends of the motif, these silk threads floated across the design like embroidered images. Koreans eventually were captivated by the glittering beauty of multi-colored, patterned weave fabrics which became very popular and seduced many people into spending fortunes on their clothing.

Kil Yong-woo in *yang-dan* hanbok by Hwang Myung-yon

Model Ringe wearing *yang-dan* (brocade) by Lee Hyo-jae

***Soo* : Embroidery**

As early as the Paleolithic and Neolithic period, people used fish-bone needles for stitchery. It is believed that most of the early embroidery art in Korea came from China along with Buddhism from Buddhist banners, and passed to Japan from Paekche culture. Before the Yi Dynasty, both men and women practiced embroidery art as an inherited profession. Evidently the skills of embroidery were well developed by the First century, during the Three Kingdoms period, but unfortunately there are no surviving examples. The oldest examples come from the late part of the Yi Dynasty. During the Yi Dynasty, the royal courts' embroidery skills reached a peak in refinement. The ceremonial robes glittered with the combination of embroidered silk and imprinted gold or silver leaf. However, it was usually accomplished by women commoners as a folk art. Korea's search for beauty continued throughout her history and is shown in all traditional folk arts and crafts, embroidery among these. Embroidery was an extremely important part of women's lives in traditional Korea. From the young age of seven women were secluded in the female quarters of the house and became embroiderers and tailors for the family's everyday wear and festive dresses. There were always plenty of special occasions for which embroidered clothes, spoon-cases, pouches, baby's socks, socks pattern holders, pillow covers, *goreum*, *daenggi* (hair ribbons), and rank badges made by women in the family of the official who wore them (or in commissioned work shops), were needed. Some of these occasions included the 100th day celebration of a baby's birth, a first birthday, a wedding, and a 60th birthday (representing the completion of the 60 year

cycle of the Asian Zodiac, a significant sign of long life).

Today, embroidery is also sewn onto folding screens, cushions, sleeping pads, jewelry boxes, curtains, and even the facade of wooden chests. The embroiderers added creative touches to their work with bright-colored threads, and by depicting auspicious symbols like the ten signs of longevity, fylfot (*man-ja*), to form the birthday wish or the greeting "Ten thousand years long life, happiness, and good luck." These recur throughout the domestic crafts of the Yi Dynasty. Usually the artisans can not be identified even though certain characteristics can be found from Yi Dynasty embroidery. There are historical references of Koguryo (37 B.C. - 668 A.D.) noble women who wore clothing embroidered with gold and silver threads. Other records show that Paekche (18 B.C. - 660 A.D.) noble women liked to wear embroidered silk clothes when they went out abroad.

Also it is recorded that during the Paekche period the technique of embroidery was transmitted to Japan. Another early record mentions that embroidered silk cloth was being sent to Tang China during the reign of Queen Chindok (647 A.D. - 54 A.D.) of Shilla. During the Unified Shilla, commoners were prohibited from wearing certain kinds of luxuriously embroidered clothing, and restrictions continued during the Koryo period (935-1392), especially if the embroidery work was related to religious patterns and ceremonies. Though the government decreed the sumptuary laws prohibiting extravagant clothing again and again, embroidery continued to be appreciated for its beauty as well as its practical uses.

Embroidered parts of bridal robe for *pyebaek* / 1680s

3

The Koryo Kingdom

The Koryo Kingdom
(918 A.D. -1392 A.D.)

Wang Kon (Taejo), one of the rebel leaders who overthrew the United Shilla, founded a new dynasty, Koryo, meaning high and clear, which was an abbreviated form of Koguryo and would later give its name of Korea to the peninsula. The third great era began in A.D. 918, with its capital city in Kaesong (Songdo). In 935, Wang Kon persuaded the last king of Shilla to surrender peacefully to Koryo which had begun in 918. Wang Kon and his successors promoted unity and harmony with all people by marrying a Shilla princess, protecting the Buddhist monks, starting a civil service system, and reorganizing the government system and freeing slaves. In the meantime, the Khitans in Mongolia established the Liao dynasty in the early part of the 10th century.

The Koryo Kingdom period was paradoxical in some ways. It was cha-racterized by repeated external threats and domestic unrest on one hand, and prosperity, cultural development, and the flow of bilateral trade with China on the other hand.

Under King Taejo a new culture began to develop in literature and ceramic art. Koryo-*tchuhngjagi*, grayish-green, olive-green, and inlaid celadon wares of the 11th and 12th centuries were graceful and elegant in shape, reaching one of the highest degrees of refinement in the world, reflecting the spirit and talent of the Koryo dynasty, and the refined taste and pleasures of Koryo aristocracy. During the 13th century, a new form of uniquely Korean pottery developed. But, unfortunately, during the Mongol invasions the secrets of Koryo celadon were lost. King Songjon (981-997 A.D.) ruled by a Confucian state model and made contacts and trade with the Song Dynasty in China. Buddhism was placed in a prominent position from the beginning of the Koryo Dynasty, members of the aristocrat class were monks, and Buddhism became the state religion. The wooden printing blocks that Shilla produced to print Buddhist texts were improved by Koryo, and Tripitaka (scriptures) were printed in the early 13th century with movable wooden printing blocks. But they were also destroyed by the Mongols. During the time when Koryo court was located in Kanghwa Island, off Inchuhn, a new set of 81,137 printing blocks was carved and in 1251 the Tripitaka Koreana was printed. These printing blocks are now preserved in the Haein Temple, and were designated as one of the World Treasures by the U.N. in 1995.

As the influence of Confucian scholars grew, historical studies increased. Among the most important works were the *Samgook Sagi* (History of the Three Kingdoms) by Kim

Simple flowing lines of Buddha's clothes can be seen.

Pu-Sik, a Confucian scholar, published in 1145, and the *Samgook Yusa* (Memorabilia of the Three Kingdoms) by Il-yon, a prominent Buddhist monk, published in 13th century. These are the most important works of historical studies and the chief sources of knowledge of early Korean history.

While Buddhism was a dominant force as a state religion in Koryo culture, Confucian influence gave structure to the society. The Khitans invaded Korea repeatedly for feudal control of the Koryo. But the entire Khitan army was destroyed by Koryo General Kang Kam-chan. Then, the Mongol Empire rose under Genghis Khan in the early 13th century, and threatened to cut Korea's ties with the Chinese. When Koryo refused to capitulate, they invaded in 1231. Koryo court moved its capital to Kanghwa Island. Six more invasions of the Mongols in the next two and half decades devastated the country. Eventually peace was made between the Mongols and Koryo, and Koryo was forced to acknowledge the feudal control of the Mongol Yuan dynasty in China, and the capital returned to Kaesong with many scars.

In the succeeding Koryo Dynasty, a peace treaty was signed with the Mongols in A.D. 1259. Korean kings were forced to marry Mongol princesses from the court of Kublai Khan, and their heirs were forced to live in Peking (Beijing) and adopt the hair style and costume of Yuan (Won) China. Three kings were born to Korean-Mongolian queens who influenced the social and costume trends of the time. The Chinese emperor sent royal robes to the Koryo kings. At the early part of the Koryo, military and civilian official costume developed with the influence of Tang, China, but from middle of the dynasty, it changed to the Yuan costume system, according to the *Haedong-suksa*, vol. 20, *Samgook Sagi*, vol. 33, *Koryo-sa* (History of Koryo) vol. 72.

Wearing *dae* of jade, leather, or cloth of the Three Kingdoms period lasted only up to the beginning of the Koryo period. Instead of the *dae,* the palace adopted the Chinese clothing and hat system to indicate rank. However, the commoners continued to wear *dae* until the *juhgori* length became shorter. Gradually the *dae* became less useful. Also, the sash at the ankle of the *buhsuhn* (cotton socks), as ornaments, disappeared during Koryo period.

The *jogdoori* (today's women's wedding crown) and *doturak-daenggi* (doubled long hair ribbon with embroideries and ornaments) were adopted Yuan Chinese

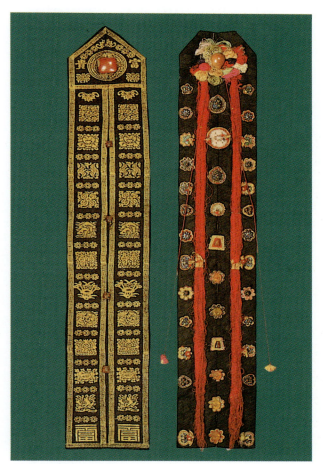

Doturak-daenggi

features and were worn until the Yi Dynasty. Commoner women wore white *guhn* (head scarves) and white clothes, but did not cover their face. Noble women wore *nuhwool* (veils), a one foot or larger black, soft silk or *sa* (stiffened silk) over a small, umbrella-like frame drawn from the crown of the head to cover their face and avoid facing the opposite sex when they went out. Social status was distinguished by the material and the size of the *nuhwool*, according to *Haedong-suksa*, vol. 20.

Official court attire was worn with *hwa* (boots), and the king wore *jucksuk* (red silk low-sided shoes with sashes) with ceremonial robes. From the time of Koryo King Wu-wang, when a new dress system was decided, black leather *hwa* was worn with official attire, until the end of the Yi Dynasty, without change. On the other hand, commoners were absolutely prohibited from wearing *hwa*, unlike the Three Kingdoms periods. Mostly they wore straw sandals, with white clothes.

Myun : Cotton

Cotton, which originally came from Mongolia, became an important development in the field of textiles and greatly improved the commoners' clothing in Korea. Cotton seeds were brought back to Korea from Yuan China in 1363 by a Korean envoy, Mun Ick-chom (1329-1398), who was sent there by Koryo King Gongmin. He gave cotton seeds for planting to his father-in-law, Chang Chan-ik, who planted and succeeded in growing them. Chang also devised a cotton gin and built a spinning wheel as well, bringing a major revolution in the Korean textile industry.

Cotton flourished throughout the country, and was a valued commodity for commoners because it provided greater warmth, and was easier and cheaper to cultivate, process, and dye than the bast fibers they had used up to that time. Cotton seeds were planted towards the end of the 3rd lunar month, and started to bloom in the middle of the 7th lunar month. After the yellowish flowers turned deep pink and were gone, green kernels grew and changed colors to light brown and eventually black. Then they opened up to reveal white cotton. This cotton was picked by hand after the 15th of the 8th lunar month, and dried on a straw mat covered with cloth under the sun. The first picked cotton was considered the finest. For cotton thread, the cotton balls were removed from the plant, seeds were extracted by hand, and the fiber was beaten. The vibration in the beating caused the cotton fibers to separate. With a small quantity of cotton connected to a spindle,

Woman resting in cotton *hanbok* who participated in folk dancing.

Nubi juhgori (quilted jacket) by Lee Young-hee

the cotton fibers were twisted into thread. After enough thread was produced, the weaving process began at the loom by using both hands. The retainment of moisture in the fiber during the weaving process of cotton as well as hemp was important, because thin fiber dries quickly and becomes brittle. This durable fabric, fine *myun* (cotton), was used for *durumagi*, *dopo* (outer coat), and a heavier *myun* was used for *baji-juhgori* and *eebul* (sleeping coverlet).

The *myun* (cotton) from Songdo (Kyong-gi-do), Chinju (Kyongsangnam-do) and Naju (Cholla-do) was considered to be the finest, and was as soft as silk. Later, upper class people also enjoyed the soft, warm, and cozy feel of fine cotton. There is a story told proudly by an elderly woman weaver, Kim Young-dong, in Tongdang-ri village, in the 1970s, who claimed that the *myun* she had woven when she was young was so fine that it was presented to the king.

During the Koryo period, the clothes of men and women were very similar in shape to the Koguryo period. The long jacket was still worn closed at the right side with long pants or skirts. More layers of *chima* were worn, and it was considered more formal for women, according to the *Koryo sa*. The queen and the wife of the prime minister wore red or purple (the supreme color), and silk robes with paintings or embroideries. But red or purple dress was not allowed for court ladies, concubines and commoners. To make *chima*, upper class women used 8 strips of lined silk. The upper class wore fine ramie for warm weather.

Court officials used yellow for their court attire. During this period the *juhgori* were shortened, the sleeves were curved slightly, and the *chima* was hiked up above the waist and tied at the chest with long sashes which hold the skirt under the *juhgori*, the same way it is worn today. Thus remains the basic *Hanbok*. Commoner women and female servants wore the same style. Men wore a hemp cloth around *sangtu* and women had hair arranged on top of their heads. Unmarried men and women began to use red or black *daenggi* (hair ribbons) again for their pigtails, instead of the string they used before, influenced by the Yuan culture at the late part of Koryo dynasty. Since there is no physical evidence of clothing of the Koryo Period, information is relied on by portraits and historical records.

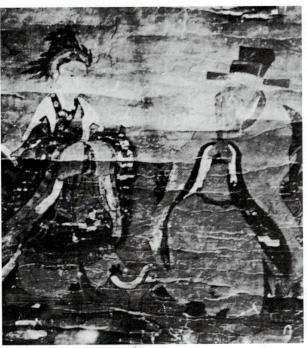

Portrait of Koryo King Gongmin (1352-1374)
Koryo / Suk Joo-sun Folk Art Museum, Seoul

Chima & *juhgori* hung on wooden hanger

The story of the portrait of the King Gongmin of Koryo (1351-1374) is that one day after the capital was moved to *Hanyang*, there was a bundle of paper dropped unexpectedly by a strong whirlwind in front of the *Jongmyo* (the ancestral temple of the royal family). It was the portrait of the King Gongmin. Ever since then, the incident was regarded as extraordinary. The portrait was installed in the *Jongmyo*, and a memorial service was performed there every year. King Gongmin is wearing a *hong-danryong* (red official robe) of extremely wide sleeves and a full length robe with black bindings around the neck line and sleeve cuffs, a girdle at the waist, and a *bok-tu* (official hat). The clothes worn by women in the picture have long and wide sleeves also. A two panel-front is opened at the center and the neckline and sleeve cuffs have small flower motifs and red bindings. A long sash is hanging down from the waist in front. The crown is in an image of a phoenix, and has many ornaments, resembling a Paekche crown excavated in July, 1971. It looks very becoming with the luxurious long dress.

Like Shilla aristocrats, Koryo upper class also indulged in extravagances and luxuries so much that King Chungjong in 1043, decreed a sumptuary law to the people who were living outside of the capital, Kaesong, which prohibited wearing clothes with the embroidery of dragon and/or phoenix motifs and gold-leaf imprints. In 1144, King Injong decreed another sumptuary law, but extravagances of the upper class continued.

As Buddhism flourished, Buddhist embroidery thrived. Some fine examples of the embroidery of the Koryo period are preserved at *Sun-am* Temple, South Cholla province today. King Gongmin of Koryo (1351-1374) officially adopted Chinese ceremonial court costumes for Korean royalty and officials soon after the Ming Dynasty in China was established (1368-1644). But Korean kings wore the costume of Chinese princes, and highest ranking officials wore the costume of Chinese third ranking officials. This court dress system lasted until the Taehan Empire, when King Gojong (1863-1907) of the Yi Dynasty declared himself emperor in 1897 and claimed empire status for Korea. Since then, the same Chinese hierarchy of court dress system has been adopted. However, Koreans always wore *hanbok* under their ceremonial outer-robe, maintaining a distinctive dual clothing system, and commoners always wore the basic *hanbok* throughout the centuries.

King Gongmin did put forth an effort to reform and restore national strength, reduce the power of the aristocrats and Buddhist monks who influenced government affairs, deal with the rising internal conflicts between Confucian teaching oriented people and the corruption of the Buddhists, and tackle the problem of the land holding system. But he also had to contend with the external threat of the northern nomads, the "Red Turbans", in the 14th century, and the frequent raids by Japanese pirates who were rampaging and plundering towns and villages along the southern and western coasts of Korea.

The armies of generals Yi Song-gye and Choe Yong drove these pirates out of Korea. However, the military efforts to defend the Kingdom drained national strength, and brought demand for yet more reform. At this difficult time, another strong leader was to appear. General Yi Song-gye in 1388 carried out a coup against the inept king, and exiled the last king of Koryo in 1392. Thus, the Koryo dynasty collapsed ending 475 years of power. Yi Song-gye then took over military and political power and declared himself king in 1392, becoming the first of the 27 rulers of the Yi Dynasty which lasted until 1910.

A hemp dress " *Yosun-tchupli* " (14th C.)

The oldest piece of intact clothing ever found in Korean history, a hemp dress, was identified as a *yosun-tchupli*, from the late Koryo period. It was one of 11 items of clothing, including *Andong-po jucksam* (jacket made of hemp produced in Andong), discovered on March 5, 1997 by a Buddhist historian, the Rev. Pomha, when he looked into the body of the Vairocana Buddha (wooden) at Haein-sa (temple) in Hapchon, South Kyongsang Province. This casual dress is believed to have been worn by a 15-year-old boy, Song Boo-gae, whose name was in a document found along with a Koryo monk's ordainment records dated 1326. The dress, *yosun-tchupli*, with a gathered waist and wing-like sleeves, was known only through records. The *tchupli* worn by the military officials of the Yi Dynasty as an outer coat, was long, gathered at the waist, and had large sleeves. However, this recent discovery, *yosun-tchupli* without large sleeves, seems like a one-piece *chima-juhgori* at first sight, giving a very contemporary appearance of beauty in style and line.

Yosun-tchupli. / 14th c.

4

The Yi Dynasty

The Yi Dynasty (Choson Kingdom) (1392-1910)

The Choson Kingdom was established by Yi Song-gye, who was given the dynastic name of Taejo. He renamed the kingdom Choson (the Land of the Morning Calm), but it was also known to western historians as the Yi Dynasty, after the family name of its founder, Yi Song-gye. He moved the capital from Kaesong (Songdo) to Seoul, and the national boundary was established along the Yalu and Tuman Rivers.

Portrait of Yi Taejo (Yi Song-gye) in *Icksungwan* (hat) and *Gon-yongpo* (king's blue silk outer robe with a medallion of a five-claw dragon on the chest, back and both shoulders indicating his Majesty's absolute dignity), and black *hwa* (velvet boots)

Korea became a tributary state of Ming China. For 500 years this dynasty knew achievement in science, music, and technology. Confucian principles guided the political and social structure of the culture as a whole, which was quite different from the Koryo Dynasty with its Buddhist-oriented aristocratic society. This was characterized through the bureaucratic structure and daily ceremony of Yi Dynasty court life, and the Chinese cosmological influence on many aspects of its life and culture. The social status of each individual was hereditary with some exceptions, but there was little upward social mobility. Strict rules and social conventions were enforced to maintain social order based on Confucianism. There were four distinctive classes: the royalty, the *yangban* (nobility), including high ranking civil and military officials and their families; the *joong-in* (middle people); the *sang-min* or *sang-in* (commoners), including tenant farmers, artisans, and merchants who paid taxes and served in the military; and the *chuhn-min* (lowborn), including public and private slaves, servants, public entertainers, shamans, Buddhist monks, butchers, gravediggers, *gisaeng* (female entertainers), and others who were thought to have unclean professions.

The Confucian Yi Dynasty emphasized practicality in life style and attitude, supporting land reform, education, and inventions. This was reflected by the simple and robust form of beauty of the *Yi-Cho-paek-jaki* (Yi-Choson-white-porcelain). In 1442 the pluviometer, a rainfall measuring device, was invented, (almost 200 years before an Italian, Gastelli, claimed its invention). King Sejong, 4th king, (1418-1450), the grandson of Yi Song-gye, developed the phonetic alphabet with 28

A 3-day celebration for a successful candidate for the civil service examination on horseback. Only sons of the *yangban* were permitted to take literary and military examinations

letters, called *Hangeul*. This was a precise and scientific writing system that was easy to learn and allowed easier expression of thought. It is still used today. Art and architecture of fine palace buildings, pavilions, and crafts were developed. Furniture makers produced beautiful, highly artistic and decorative furniture, which has been treasured by people around the world. The Yi Dynasty knew great achievement and glory, and maintained peace for its first two hundred years. Confucianism became the official guiding principle, suppressing Buddhism, (although the private practice of Buddhism continued, even in the court).

Quietly, Buddhist monks built new religious centers, creating beautiful and imposing temples in remote areas of the mountains away from the capital city, and continued their devotion.

In 1592, disaster struck the Yi Dynasty when Toyotomi Hideyoshi of Japan invaded the Korean peninsula, captured the capital, and took over almost the entire peninsula. Admiral Yi Sun-sin, with his war 'turtle ships', won a tremendous victory against the Japanese, cutting off supply lines from Japan. However, in 1597, the Japanese sent an army again to Korea and fighting renewed. Meanwhile, Ming Dynasty Chinese troops arrived to assist the Koreans, and the combined forces managed to block the Japanese. Finally, at the end of 1597, with the death of Toyotomi Hideyoshi, the Japanese invaders withdrew from Korea. But the fighting had taken its toll on Korea. The Japanese invaders had destroyed historical buildings, killed hundreds of thousands of people, taken hundreds of captured potters, farmers, and skilled workers to Japan, while leaving their families behind, and ravaged and despoiled the whole country.

The damages on Korea from this long war were so severe that it became the greatest disaster in Korea's history. Subsequently, normal relations between Korea and Japan were not fully restored until 1876.

In 1627 and 1636 the Manchu Empire, named Later Chin from Manchuria, invaded the completely unprepared Yi dynasty, and demanded that the Manchu Empire become Korea's superior.

The first European to Korea arrived in 1627. A Dutchman, Jan Janse Weltevree, and his two companions were captured at shore while their ship fled from Korea, and were kept in Korea to produce weapons and train Korean troops. In July 1653 a Dutch ship, Sparrow Hawk, was shipwrecked near Cheju Island in the south of Korea, and Hendrik Hamel with some 30 crew members was rescued by the Koreans but kept as a spy. Hamel escaped from Korea with some of his crew and published the first Western book on Korea in 1668 in Holland, introducing Korea to European and Western countries.

Basic *Hanbok*

Throughout the centuries during the Confucian Yi Dynasty, with its strict emphasis on etiquette and manners, the form and style of Korean dress developed. This resulted in a distinctive style of clothing known as *hanbok*, which has been worn by Koreans at least since the Three Kingdoms period. The rigid dress code was decided according to status and rank, based on Confucian hierarchy for the emperor, empresses, kings, queens, government officials, gentlemen scholars, and people born of low class. The system of ceremonial robes of the court of the Yi Dynasty was modeled after the Ming China's system, which was brought by Hwang-um, during the reign of King Taejong in 1403.

For traditional ceremonies, a specific dress for a particular occasion was stipulated. One style of dress for a certain ceremonial occasion could never be worn at another time, indicative of the Yi Dynasty life style. However, they always wore, under the ceremonial robe, traditional *chima-juhgori* for women and *baji-juhgori* for men.

With the numerous prohibitions and sumptuary laws decreed with almost every new king, during the Yi Dynasty, clothing became simpler, forming the *Hanbok* of today. The costume materials varied with the change of season, cut and length of the *juhgori* went up and down with fashion and social standing, and individual's ranks, class, sex, and age were distinguished by specific colors, lengths and styles.

The muted colors for the every day wear of commoners, and the splendid, vibrant, finery of court costume was a deliberate statement of the absolute authority of the royal household.

Juhgori : Jacket

The long jackets of the Three Kingdoms period gradually changed to extremely short ones for women as shown in an 18th century genre paintings by Shin Yun-bok (born in 1758- , Kansong Art Museum) or Yi In-moon. Also the neckline closed more tightly and higher than the today's lower openings.

Men's *baji* & *juhgori* have changed very little.

The beauty and quality of a *hanbok* was judged by the curve of the sleeves, and the way the collar, called a *git*, and the *sup* (front gusset of the *juhgori*) ended, and was attached by the *goreum* to tie at the right side of the chest. This created an interesting accent to the simple style of the *juhgori*.

The *dongjuhng* was a white narrow neckband, stiffened with paper underneath, and stitched over the *git* (collar), forming a sharp restrained neckline. The *dongjuhng* was often detached and replaced. It was very cleverly designed. Because it had direct contact with the neck it often got dirty. So it was easily removed from the jacket and

Jogagbo (silk patch-work with embroidery)
60 x 60 cm. / 1933 / by Park Hyung-ja

replaced with a new one to economize cleaning and expense. When the whole ensemble needed cleaning, they took apart each worn piece, washed it by hand, then ironed and restitched it with new thread.

Sometimes, after many wearings, the fabric was inverted for better color and new strength, then restitched all over with new thread. The used threads were saved for non-critical stitching, such as basting. Eventually, after years of wearing and washing, the clothes were cut up for further use, such as patchwork for wrapping cloths. If it was cotton or hemp, then it became soft enough to use as diapers for a baby's delicate skin. Finally, these leftovers were used as cleaning rags.

The cleaning task for clothing made of ramie was extremely time consuming. All ramie clothing had to be pounded with a heavy wooden stick on a smooth, shiny, rectangular stone base in order to release the starch in the ramie, which would then give a crisp, glossy texture to the dry garment. No longer can one hear the rhythmic sounds of pounding ramie from the neighbors in the late evening hours as heard in years gone by.

The *goreum* (two ribbons) for the *juhgori* and *durumagi* was introduced sometime before the 15th century. The *juhgori* was side-fastened with a *git* (broad collar) edge crossing to the wearer's right, and was secured internally by left-fastening small inner ribbons, one at the edge of the left armpit, the other at the edge of the right collar. The *juhgori* overlapped on the left side at the outside and tied by right-fastening, larger, longer tie ribbons, *goreum*, which were different from the butterfly like bows of the west. The *goreum* played a prominent role not only for the practical purpose of keeping *juhgori* closed in place, but also as an ornamental ribbon for females, often embellished with silver or gold leaf imprints, or with embroidery of auspicious motifs.

Samhoejang juhgori were only worn by upper class women (*yangban*) in earlier periods of the Yi Dynasty. Commoners were allowed to wear *ban-hoejang juhgori*. To avoid the uniformity of a standard cut of *juhgori*, a contrasting colored material was applied on the *git, goreum*, sleeve cuffs, and *giyut-magi* (armpit insertions).

Reddish purple was a common choice for this purpose, but indigo blue may also have been applied on the cuffs. This embellished the simplicity of the *juhgori*, and added a sense of refreshing color harmony.

Wooden sticks and stone base used to pound clothes
19th c.

57

Quilted *myungju* (silk) women's jacket
L. 58 cm
W. of sleeves. 75.5 cm.
17th C.
Ewha Womans Univ. Museum, Seoul.

Princess Dogon's yellow, quilted silk with a white lining, very short in length, with very narrow and long sleeves *juhgori* (1837)
Suk Joo-sun Memorial Folk Art Museum, Seoul.

Quilted violet *juhgori* of Emperor Gojong
1864-1907
Suk Joo-sun Folk Art Museum, Seoul.

Women's green *sa* (stiffened silk gauze) *juhgori*
L. 24 cm
W. of sleeves. 63 cm.
1920.
Ewha Womans Univ. Museum, Seoul.

Yellow was most often selected for the *juhgori*. It was worn with indigo blue silk skirts, woven with auspicious motifs of Chinese characters for happiness, good luck, long life, and flowers with scrolling vines, and amply pleated to create an elegant silhouette. This combination was considered an appropriate ensemble for a dignified, upper class married lady.

As Yi Dynasty upper class women wore fewer jewels than Shilla aristocrats, a *norigae* (pendant of gold, semiprecious stones) hung from the *goreum* or skirt sash, and hair was decorated with *binyuh* (crossbar), *dwitkkoji* (small beautiful hair pins), and rings completed the attire for special events. Yellow *juhgori* with crimson red *chima*s were for unmarried young women, and bright green *juhgori* with crimson red *chima* for newly wedded young women. Married women wore yellow *juhgori* with blue *chima*, which is still practiced today.

Ban-hoejang juhgori, worn by commoners, did not have *giyut-magi* (armpit insertions of contrasting colors). Based on a strict class distinction, the Yi Dynasty social norm did not allow women of all classes to enjoy many variations of fashion, however minor they may have been. Thus the *ban-hoejang juhgori* was an alternative for the common women, as their skirts were unlined and shorter, so that under-garments showed, to indicate lower status.

Just as today's high fashion often strays toward the risqué and is rejected by the "establishment", so too did this happen in the Yi Dynasty. There was a time when married women were often seen in extremely different *juhgori* which had protruding neckbands, and were severely squared at the edge with very narrow and short *goreum*. Sleeves were extremely narrow, tight-fitting, and the length of the *juhgori* was so short that the chestband of the skirt showed almost entirely. This was considered very undignified by conservative Koreans. This short small style of *juhgori* became the subject of criticism and was disapproved for its vulgar fashion, and gradually disappeared.

Chima : Skirt

The *chima* was the other part of the basic two piece clothing set. These traditional Korean women's skirts were ample, full, and high waisted, so that body lines were completely concealed, giving beauty to the form by its silhouette. Unlike western clothing, with exact standard sizes which were measured and cut to fit to the body as closely as possible, Korean clothing used more general measurements by structuring it to wrap around the body and fasten with sashes. The *chima* had no waist size and no specific length. The *chima* was attached to a white cotton chestband which wrapped

Red silk skirt

Lady Han's *seuran chima*
Silk woven with gold thread in motifs of grapes and young boys
L. 103 cm / W. 504cm
18th C.
Suk Joo-sun Folk Art Museum, Seoul

around the body at the chest under the armpit, and tied in front by a smaller and narrower sash that was attached at both ends of the chestband, under the *juhgori*.

The *chima* came in one size which could be adjusted simply by loosening or tightening its sash. This was the same with the *juhgori*, which could be adjusted by the *goreum*, and men's *baji* which adjusted at the front-fold and waist sash. The *chima* with many pleats was not only easy for the movement of the wearer, but also it emphasized the opulence and elegance of Korean women. It also made the wearer look taller and more graceful in every movement. Whether sitting, rising, or walking, there was a constant flow of colorful material which was very pleasing.

Unlike the western style skirt which was worn in one method, the Korean *chima*, besides being worn at the chest, could become a *bojagi* (wrapper), *dotjari* (mat when spread out for sitting), *cha-il* (sunshade or blind), *podaegi* (coverlet), *jang-ot* (head-cover, worn by Korean women when they went out in the earlier period in Korea), as well as a flag which hung on a pole. Most of the *chima-hwiho* (writing, painting, and drawing done on the outer or inner skirt) has been collected, made into folding screens, and exhibited. The prominent and frequent visitor to a *gisaeng* house (professional female entertainers who are well versed in poetry, and trained in calligraphy, music, and painting) would leave *chima-hwiho* to a particular *gisaeng* with whom he had a romantic relationship, either as a proposal, as an ending gift, or as payment for his drinks. The *gisaeng* would take off her *chima* and spread it out requesting the honor of his *hwiho* as an expression of her love toward that particular guest, or as a proposal gesture. A well known *hwiho* was done in gratitude by the Heung-sun Taewon-gun, Yi Ha-ung, father of the King Gojong (r. 1863), on an inner skirt of Tchu-sun, a *gisaeng*, who helped him obtain secret information from the court.

Under the outer skirt women wore *sok-chima* (slips), *sok-baji* (culottes) or *dan-sok-ot* (pantaloons) and/or *gojaeng-ee* (a kind of petticoat). They also wore a shorter, smaller, unlined, *sok-jucksam* (inner jacket).

The *juhgori* (jacket) of matching or contrasting color and material balanced well in proportion with *chima* (skirt). The *chima* could enhance the nice figure of women and also could conceal those figures not so fully blessed. With *juhgori*, one could wear the collar long and narrow, to make the neck appear longer, or wear it wide and short, to make the neck appear shorter. A nursing mother could easily arrange her *juhgori* to accommodate breast feeding her child.

Women of the Confucian-oriented Yi Dynasty began to wear wraparound, full, pleated *chima* and longer *juhgori* in the 15th century. The women of the *yangban* wore wrap-around, full-length, *chima* that were about a foot (30 cm.) longer than normal skirts and had many more pleats to indicate their social status. In contrast, the commoners were prohibited from wearing *chima* of more than 10 or 12 *pok* (*pok*- width of strips of cloth) and were required to over-lap them on the right side, which was the opposite of the *yangban chima*. The *yangbans'* full skirt was called *gudeul-chima*. There was a slight inconvenience for this extra long and full, elegant silk skirt when activity was involved. It was good only for the sedentary life styles of nobility. They would pull up the skirt from the waist and tie it with long, indigo blue silk sashes over the jacket at the chest. This required some maneuvering, putting the right hand under the skirt, pulling the skirt over the short jacket from left to right to make a large gathering, then using the left hand from the outside to let the gathering spread evenly, and then tying it with the sash. Then they had to readjust the length of the skirt. But as fashion trends began to shorten the *juhgori* until it just covered the breasts, it was necessary to reduce the fullness of the *chima* so that it could be easily extended to the armpits. Today's *Hanbok* are patterned after those worn by women of the *yangban* during the Yi Dynasty.

Since Korea has four distinct seasons, clothing was made accordingly. The colors and materials used varied according to the wearer's social status, wealth, sex, age and taste. At the turn of the century, when women started going to school and working outside the home, they had their skirt gathered less fully, and made it into a shorter (mid-calf length), tube-like skirt which did not wrap around, in darker and subdued colors. The gathered skirt was held at the chest by an unlined, vest-like, top part (like a high-waisted, sleeveless one-piece dress) for wearing under the *juhgori*. It was called a *tong-chima* (tube-skirt). Both styles of skirts are worn today.

Beautiful *chima* with *geum-bak* & *juhgori*

Official Dress for Men

From the age of seven, men of the Yi Dynasty court were sent to *suhdang* (private school) to prepare to become high ranking civil and military officials. Officials were required to wear appropriate dresses for various ceremonies. Their dresses were embellished with elaborate embroidery and gold-leaf imprints of auspicious symbols on splendid garments. The rank of officials were indicated by the length and color of the robe, width of sleeves, woven designs on the silk material used for robe, their emblematic badges on the robe, *hol* (tablet carried by hands), *dae* (girdle, stick-hoop-like belt), shoes of the different material, and number of gold stripes on the crown.

Dress of the Emperor (or King)

Gujangbok : Ceremonial Robe with Nine Symbols

Gujangbok or *myun-bok* was the king's or emperor's full court robe which was worn on ceremonial occasions. The great ceremonial robe with nine symbols has been worn by kings from the time of King Gongmin (1351-1374) of Koryo Kingdom, and has been enacted to higher ranking *ship-eejang-bok* (with twelve symbols) since King Gojong (1863-1907) proclaimed Korea's empire status. (It became the independent 'Great Han Empire' in October, 1897, and he became an emperor.)

This robe was worn when performing sacrificial rites at the Royal Ancestral Shrine,

Black silk gauze *gujangbok*
19th c. / Yi Royal Family Museum, Seoul

Gujangbok and *myunyugwan*.
20th c.

62

Jongmyo. The wide sleeved robe was made of patterned black silk gauze, *sa*, and lined with red or dark blue silk.

It had a distinctive white wide neck band, fastened at the right side of the chest with *goreum*, and was bordered with the same color and material on the collar, sleeves, front opening, hem, and embellished with nine auspicious symbols for the king and twelve for the emperor, indicating the power of the ruler as an intermediary between heaven and earth. Only the emperor could wear all twelve symbols which, when placed on a robe, assumed cosmic significance and signified the emperor as the Ruler of the Universe. ※

※
  Dragon for majesty and supernatural power
  Mountain peaks for stability and pacification
  Flames for one of five primary elements
  Pheasants for its splendid beauty
  Sacrificial wine cups for filial piety
  Grains of millet or rice for cultivation and nutrition
  Axes for decisiveness and judgment
  Clouds for rain and dew for human benefit
  Key frets for devotion and the forces of good and evil
  Bullocho for longevity
  Fylfot for discrimination or 10,000 cheers
  Sun and moon for primary elements

The *gujangbok* was worn over an inner robe, *joong-dan*, which was worn over *juhgori* and *baji*. A *pyeseul* (front apron) was attached in the front, and a *hoosoo* (back apron) with white jade on both sides was draped on the back of the robe. This austere looking robe, with elaborate accessories, completed the formal attire. An *okdae* (girdle with white jade plaques) or a *bichwi-dae* (girdle with green jade plaques) was worn around the chest, and the king held an *ok-gyu* (white jade *hol*, tablet) in both his hands, and on his feet he wore a pair of leggings, red socks, and *jucksuk* (red silk shoes).

Myunyugwan : Mortarboard hat

The *myunyugwan* was worn with the ceremonial robe, as ceremonial headgear, by the emperor. This tradition, originated from the Zhou (Chu) dynasty of China. The *myunyugwan* and *myun-bok* (ceremonial robes) were worn as the court attire for royal ancestral memorial services, ceremonies honoring Heaven and Earth, the guardian deities of the state and agriculture, and ennoblement and enthronement ceremonies. Rank was indicated by the decorations on the *myunyugwan*. In 1897, when Emperor Gojong ascended the throne, the same system as Ming China was adopted. Twelve pendants of beads for the

Myunyugwan for the emperor.
Black outside, red inside, mortarboard in brown.
W. 34cm. / L. 41cm. / H. 12cm.
1958 (reproduction).
Suk Joo-sun Museum, Seoul

Emperor, nine pendants for the king, seven for the crown prince, five for his son, and three for high ranking officials were worn.

The front of the hat was round and lowered, and the back was raised. The hat was topped with a flat mortar board. The surface was covered with black silk and lined with red silk. Nine pendants hung in the front and back, each pendant with nine beads in five colors of red, white, blue, yellow, black, or green. The pendants covered the eyes to prevent the king from seeing undesirable sights. The purple silk cords or ribbons with jade beads were attached at both sides, covering the ears, preventing the king from hearing undesirable talk, and tied under the chin.

Jucksuk : Red silk ceremonial shoes for the king

Jucksuk was worn by King Gongmin (1351-1374) of Koryo in 1370 with his ceremonial robe. According to the 'Koryo History', these red shoes were made of stiffened layers of paper or cotton and leather, and a low-sided, upper part was covered with red silk damask, hand-sewn with red silk thread, and outlined around the edges of the shoes with a thin cord made of red silk threads. A long, red silk sash was attached that was looped at the instep and heel to tie around the ankle over red or white *buhsuhn*, and decorated with dark red or gold couching, and blue or wine colored silk tassels at the toes. But, during the Yi Dynasty, according to the *Hong-moo Yaejae* (King Hong-moo ceremony system), in the 26th year of King Hong-moo (1393), the kings began to wear the red silk shoes again, and from then on kings and crown princes wore *jucksuk* trimmed in blue or red silk sashes, which tied at the ankle, with their ceremonial robes.

Hwang-yongpo : Emperor's Yellow Dragon Robe

When Korea's ruler first used the title of emperor in 1887, toward the end of the Yi Dynasty, the emperor wore *hwang-yongpo* when carrying out official duties. The yellow robe was made of a fine cloud patterned silk brocade, lined with soft, red

Jucksuk. / 26 x 7.5cm./ 19th c. / The Elcanto Co. coll.

King Gojong in *hwang-yongpo* / 19th c
Suk Joo-sun Folk Art Museum, Seoul

silk in the winter, and *sa* without lining in the summer. (It was also called *gon-yongpo* and was sometimes made in indigo blue). The round neckline was closed at the right shoulder and tied by a *goreum* on the right side of the chest. The *bo* (emblematic medallion of a five-clawed dragon embroidered in gold) was attached on the chest, back, and shoulders.

Wearing an *icksungwan* (hat) with this robe began from the time of King Sejong (1418-1450). *Icksungwan* was a round, black, lacquered gauze, double-crested hat with two upright, small, wing-like flaps in back, symbolizing a queen bee, which is known for being in good order and of strict discipline. A jade *dae* and *mok-hwa* (black deer skin boots) were worn.

Princes and their sons wore this robe when they were young in *jajuk-yongpo* (purplish red robe) with a *gong-jung-chaek* (purple hat). The Crown Prince wore *bo* with a four-clawed dragon, and his son wore *bo* of a three-clawed dragon. *Icksungwan*, *okdae* (jade girdle), *sang-ah-hol* (ivory tablet) and *mok-hwa* (black felt boots) completed the attire. But the Crown Prince and emperor's brother wore *wonyugwan* (purple, silk, cylinder-shaped hat with a spiral pattern on each side) with this robe.

Icksungwan.
Black horse hair.
19th c.
Suk Joo-sun Folk Art Museum, Seoul

Okdae Girdle with jade plaques
19th c.
Suk Joo-sun Folk Art Museum, Seoul

Mok-hwa.
Black felt boots.
19th c.
Suk Joo-sun Folk Art Museum, Seoul

※ The dragon was an imaginary animal known for its innumerable changes of behavior and considered the king of all animals. Therefore it symbolized the absolute power of the king and emperor. The dragon, like the phoenix, was used as an emblem of nobility and power. The face of a king was called the dragon face (*yong-an*) and his royal costume the dragon robe (*yong-po*). Legend has it that a giant golden carp from the deep ocean transformed into a yellow dragon. So, the imperial robe and throne are yellow brocade embroidered with golden threads. The legendary dragon rose into the sky on his chariot of clouds behind a veil of thick fog and gave rain to the earth for the benefit of human beings. As no one had seen the dragon's face, it was forbidden to look on the face of the celestial emperor or king, and all subjects were commanded to bow to him.

Hong-yongpo : King's Red Official Robe

The red silk robe *hong-yongpo*, (also called *gangsapo*), was worn over the *joong-dan* (inner robe) which was worn over *juhgori-baji*. There were front *pyeseul* (front apron, knee cover), *hoosoo* (embroidered silk back apron), and *hyoong-dae*. Jade pendants suspended on both sides from the waist, and an *ok-hol* (jade tablet) was held by both hands. *Mok-hwa*, and *wonyu-gwan* which were less formal than the *myunyugwan*, completed the court attire of the king for audiences.

Hong-yongpo was for the kings and the crown princes when they were carrying out official duties. The robe was made of red silk satin or cloud patterned brocade, lined with soft, blue silk for winter, and unlined red *sa* for summer, with a white neckband, fastening at the right with a long *goreum* at the right side of the chest. It had wide, long sleeves. The emblematic medallion with a five-clawed dragon was attached only on the back and front of the robe for the king.

Wonyugwan was the ceremonial headgear of court attire. The *jobok* (courtiers formal attire) was worn on New Year's Day, winter solstice, and at state and royal functions. The hat was covered and lined with silk and decorated with strings of beads of five colors between silk cords, which indicated rank by the number. It originated from Ming China's crown *pi-bian*. This ridged hat of woven rattan covered with gauze and a hairpin was worn with military attire, while a black, silk gauze hat with 12 ridges, decorated with gold thread, beads, and a jade hairpin was worn with formal attire. In the late Yi Dynasty, the 12-ridge system was adopted along with a jade hair pin and red ribbons fastened under the chin.

A portrait of King Gojong (r. 1863-1907)
Royal Museum in Duksoo Palace, Seoul

Hyoong-dae of jade worn by the Yong-Wang, which is covered with red cloud patterned silk, decorated with round jade plaques, and fastened by a dragon motif, carved, square, jade buckle. 114cm.
19th c.
The Yi Dynasty

Red *wonyugwan*.
H. 22cm.
1890.
Oryudae Hankook Sunkyoja Memorial Hall.

Hong-yongpo worn by the regent, Daewon-goon.
Suk Joo-sun Museum, Seoul

68 Scene of the court banquet on the folding screen (1901) by Kim Hong-do (Danwon) / National Museum, Seoul

◐ *Young-Wang* : **The Last Crown Prince**

In October 1991, Japan returned to Korea the costumes worn by the last Crown Prince, King (*wang*) *Young* of the Daehan Empire, the 3rd son of Emperor Gojong (1863-1907), his Japanese wife Bangja, and their son Jin-Wangja. These costumes not only provided important details and information about royal family costumes of the Yi Dynasty, but also had great historical significance. Emperor Gojong was forced by the Japanese to abdicate the throne, thus ending Korea's Empire status. The Crown Prince, Young-Wang, abdicated in 1907 and was taken to Japan in 1908 by the Japanese as a hostage at age 11. There he was forced to marry a Japanese noble woman, Bangja, in 1920.

In April 1922, royal costumes were prepared in Korea for the Crown Prince Young-Wang, his wife Bangja, and their son Jin-Wangja to wear during their first visit to Korea since the abduction. They were to have an audience with King Soon-jong (1907-1910), the first son of Emperor Gojong and elder brother of Young-Wang, who abdicated in 1910 under Japanese pressure. In addition, they made courtesy offerings to the ancestral memorials of previous kings, participating in traditional rites, in proper costumes.

Hong-yongpo (red silk satin robe) worn by the Young-Wang.
189 x 130cm. / 19th c.
Duksoo palace Museum, Seoul

Hong-wonsam (ceremonies and weddings for Queen Bangja).
The borders were woven in gold.
Red, silk brocade woven in cloud and dragon motifs, and lined with yellow silk.
262 x 156.5cm.
Duksoo Palace Museum, Seoul

These costumes and accessories of the Yi royal court, in original form, are in excellent condition and of great variety. They are among the most complete and valuable relics of all existing royal costumes, and are important historical objects for future research. Included are the ceremonial robes, *hong-yongpo* (red silk robe with dragon medallion) for the Crown Prince, *geumjik-dang-ui* (silk robe woven in gold), *juhg-ui* (blue silk robe with pheasant embroidery for an empress), *wonsam* (for ceremonies and weddings) for Bangja, and *jajuk-yongpo* (red silk outer robe with dragon medallion), *sakyu-sam* (green silk robe with open sides), and *durumagi* (outer robe) for the royal grandson, Jin-Wangja, and as well as everyday wear. The accessories included are the *gachae* (wig), *geumjik-daenggi* (hair ribbons with gold imprints), *bong-jam* (cross bar with phoenix decorations at one end), *yong-jam* (with dragon decorations), and *norigae* (pendants) of high artistic quality. The shoes, accessories, and head gear, confirm the documented records of 500 years of the Yi Dynasty costume.

A woman wearing a cross bar

Yong-jam (a cross bar with a dragon at the one end, worn with wig for great ceremonies and wedding).
L. 26cm
Duksoo Palace Museum, Seoul

Jookjam (with bamboo design).
L. 21cm
Duksoo Palace Museum, Seoul

Juhg-ui (great ceremonial blue silk brocade robe with embroideries) for Queen, Bangja.
208. x 153.5cm. / Duksoo Palace Museum, Seoul

Ttuljam decorated with gem stones on a different base.
Delicate fluttering effects are the characteristic of these hair pins for Queen Bangja.
White Jade base, gold, ruby, sapphire and pearls.
L. 12cm.
Duksoo Palace Museum, Seoul

Danghye (silk covered leather shoes for Queen Bangja)
It is decorated on the toes and heels by green silk in a cloud motif.
Red silk *damsa* woven in peony motif in silver.
L. 26 x 5.5cm
Duksoo Palace Museum, Seoul

Dang-ui (for minor ceremonies for Queen Bangja).
Green, silk brocade with gold-leaf imprints all over the jacket.
It was also worn by noble women for major ceremonies and weddings.
145 x 83.6cm.
Duksoo Palace Museum, Seoul

Geumbak-daeran chima (formal skirt for Queen Bangja).
Dark blue large silk brocade skirt with gold-leaf imprints.
324 x 142cm.
Duksoo Palace Museum, Seoul

Duru-joomuhni (King Young's round silk wish-pouch for well-being and peace) embroidered with 5 different colored silk threads, and used gold thread for the border.
11.5cm. / Duksoo Palace Museum, Seoul

※ In Yi court it was a custom that the pouch with yellow beans put inside, was given to ministers by the king to drive out an evil spirit.

So-bong-jam (small hair pin of a phoenix design to be worn on both sides of a big wig when wearing *juhg-ui* for Queen Bangja.
Gold, ruby, sapphire and pearl.
L. 19cm.
Duksoo Palace Museum, Seoul

Norigae given to Queen Bangja by the wife of Ui-Wang (Young-Wang's elder brother) in 1941 as a typical wedding gift. Worn on the chest, and considered a valuable heirloom
L. 29.5cm .
Duksoo Palace Museum, Seoul

a. Coral and gold
b. Twin jade butterfly, gold, ruby, green jade and pearls
c. *Ja mano* (amethyst agate) in the shape of bat. All with knots in chrysanthemum shape and tassels
Duksoo Palace Museum, Seoul

Heuk-yongpo : Casual black robe for the Crown Prince

The casual attire of the Crown Prince consisted of a black silk outer robe with a four-clawed dragon emblematic medallion, an *icksungwan* (winged black hat which was constructed with multi-layered paper and covered with black silk), an *okdae* (girdle decorated with jade plaques), a pair of white cotton socks and leggings, and *mok-hwa* (mid-calf length, black felt covered, leather boots).

The black silk outer robe was made of *sa* (patterned silk gauze), lined with red silk, and bordered in black. The robe had a round collar showing the white neck band of the *juhgori* worn underneath, large sleeves fastened with red and black *goreum* at the right side, and an emblematic medallion with a four-clawed dragon, *bo* (3 clawed dragon for the eldest son) was attached on the shoulders, front, and back.

Jajuk-yongpo : Magenta ceremonial robe for Royal Grandson, *Jin-wangja*

A beautifully shaped *jajuk-yongpo* (magenta silk brocade ceremonial robe) with round emblematic medallions of a three-clawed dragon with gold-leaf imprints was made for Young-Wang's son, the Royal grandson Jin-Wangja. He was born in 1921 and visited King Soonjong in Korea with his parents in April 1922 when he was 7 months old. The robe has a curved round neck line, collar, and inner and outer *goreum* of the same color and material. However, it has never been worn.

Jajuk-yongpo for the Royal Grandson.
Magenta patterned silk brocade.
98 x 69cm.
19th c.
The Yi Dynasty

Sakyu-sam : Green outer robe

The *sakyu-sam* was for the Royal grandson, Jin-Wangja, to wear over the *hong-po* (red *durumagi*). It was made of light green softer silk brocade woven in a peony pattern, bordered with black silk brocade with gold-leaf imprints in various auspicious symbols and Chinese characters, and a curved collar. It was held at end of the collar by buttons, and reveals the *hong-po* with a white neck band worn inside.

Sakyu-sam for Jin Wangja to be worn over the red robe.
Green shimmering soft silk brocade, woven in a peony motif, and decorated with gold-leaf imprints and black borders.
92.6 x 68.4cm
19th c.
Duksoo Palace Museum, Seoul

Bo : Emblematic Medallions for the Royal Family

Throughout Korea's recorded history, the aristocrats' and the courtiers' clothing was determined by official ranks. The 'Great Code of Administration' of 1485 proclaimed specific instructions about the clothes, as well as the insignia badges to be worn by civil and military officials at various ceremonies in the court of the Yi Dynasty.

The *bo* were usually made of exquisite silk of the same material and color as the robe on which the *bo* were attached. Auspicious symbols were embroidered, basted with rice paper, lined with silk, and attached on the shoulders, chest, and back of the formal robes of the royal family during the Yi Dynasty. The *yong-bo* (emblematic medallion with the four-clawed dragon motif) was first worn by King Sejong in 1446 (year 26). As Korea's rulers began to use the title of emperor in 1897, toward the end of the Yi Dynasty, the emperor wore *geumsu-ojo-yong-bo* (a five-clawed dragon motif embroidered with gold thread on his royal emblematic medallion).

The design of the emperor's 24 scalloped medallion was rendered in gold embroidery in single or double stitches. With this was a design of a red flame from *yuh-uiju* (a magic stone that bestows omnipotence on he who acquires it) and a sun in between the face of the dragon and body.

The empress's *hwang-wonsam* (yellow ceremonial robe) was embellished with an identical emblem. But her *dang-ui* (outer-jacket) for semi-ceremonial occasions had emblematic squares, instead of medallions, of a phoenix design in the same material and color as the jacket, on the chest and back. But the *dang-ui* worn by Princess Dogon, the 3rd daughter of King Soonjong, had a medallion.

The Crown Prince and his wife were allowed a four-clawed dragon design with a red flame between the face of the dragon and body, without the sun motif, on their emblematic medallions. The grandson had a three-clawed dragon with a thicker mane, youthful facial expression, and a fuller scale of the dragon, showing energy, power, and strength, evoking its mystical feeling.

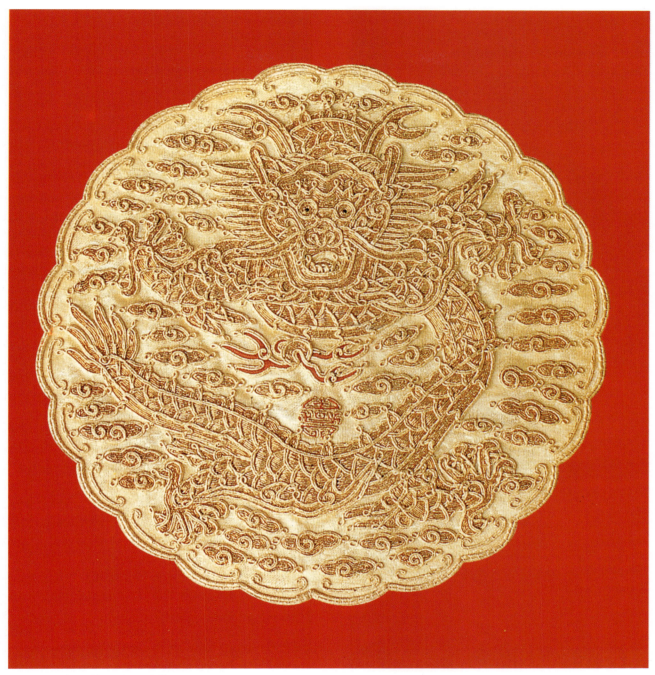

Bo (emperor's emblematic medallion).
Yellow silk brocade.
Gold and red embroidery of 5-clawed dragon.
19. 5 cm. dia.
1850
Woon-hyun Palace Museum, Seoul

※ The face of the dragon, and the front & back claws look like an old lion, and the body resembles a scaled snake.

It was believed in ancient times that the sky was round and the earth square. The ultimate power of the king was compared to the heavens. Thus *bo* (medallion) were for the royal family, and the *hyoongbae* (square insignia) were for the courtiers.

Bo (for empress or queen).
Reddish purple silk satin for *jugh-ui* & *wonsam*.
Embroidered with gold and 5 different color silk threads.
18.5 cm. dia. / 1850s.

※ On a reddish purple background the dragon with 5-claws is surrounded by the longevity symbols (mountains, rocks, waves) and the seven treasures (gold, silver, lapis, crystal, coral, jade, pearls) in colors. It is outlined with two lines of gold thread, not scalloped, but in a plain circle.

Dress of the *Yangban* (upper class)

The *yangban*, the members of the two orders of officialdom who served in the bureaucracy of the Yi Dynasty (the Choson Kingdom, 1392-1910), were the privileged class which held civil and military posts based on scholarship and official position rather than on wealth. These aristocratic Confucian scholar-gentlemen spent their days memorizing the Analects of Confucius, composing poetry, and practicing calligraphy, besides their official duties. Their room, *sarangbang*, was near the gate of their house, and was used exclusively either as a study, for entertaining guests, or for sleeping when they were not with their wife or concubine. It was an *ondol* room which was simple, dignified and serene, and was furnished with wooden chests for clothing and books, a desk, and *chaekgori* (book chest) made of paulownia wood. The corner chests were for their collections of favorite objects of art such as celadon, bronze vessels and lacquerware, all luxury items. They treasured the utensils of their academic pursuits, such as rolls of rice paper, writing brushes, inkstones and ink-sticks. These were called the "Four Friends of the Scholar", and were stored in 'inkstone boxes' or in the *moon-gap*, a long low chest which usually had four doors, each with white brass plum flower designed ornaments and drawers. A fine folding screen with *chaekgori* paintings was placed behind a scholar's desk. *Yangban*s preferred simple elegance. Besides furniture, there was a *boryo* (silk covered large cushion), and armrests covered with the same material as the cushions with embroideries, kerosene lamps on tall standing holders, a small brazier (*hwaro*) with teapots and cups for tea, an incense burner, an ash tray, a long bamboo smoking pipe, a pipe-holder, a tobacco case, seals, an eyeglass with a case, and fans. A scroll of ink drawings or calligraphy in muted hues (unlike those in bright colors which hung in women's rooms) on the wall, a *badook* (go game) board, and a musical instrument, since music was cultivated by Confucian gentlemen, reflected the taste, beliefs, and the financial status of the master of the house.

Also there were potted miniature plants (*boonjae*) and polished rock collections. All this conveyed an air of dignity, luxury and scholarship.

*Yangban*s' wives were secluded in the ladies quarters of the walled compounds where three to five generations lived together. It was considered rude beyond measure, for *yangban* gentleman guests even to ask after the health of his host's wife.

● *Sarangchae* : Men's Quarters

There were strict regulations governing the size and structure of the house in accordance with the status of the owner. But a typical Korean house consisted of inner and outer quarters and rooms. The *an-bang* (inner rooms) were the women's rooms in the *anchae* (inner quarter) or women's quarter, and the *sarangbang* (outer room) were the men's rooms in the men's quarter. In larger families, the master of the house occupied the *keun* (larger) *sarangbang* and the eldest son used the *jageun* (smaller) *sarangbang*. Parents of the master of the house would use another detached building called *an-sarang* (inner sarang).

Sliding paper doors usually divided rooms into two parts. The walls and ceilings were covered with rice paper of white or pale grayish blue, and the heated *ondol* floor was covered with oiled paper.

Jobok : Official Court Attire

The civil and military high ranking officials (3rd rank or above) wore the *jobok* for the morning audience with the king and other ceremonial events. The ensemble consisted of a fine, red silk gauze robe worn over a blue inner robe, and a similar red silk apron

Jobok.
Red, silk outer robe: 94 x 190cm.
Blue, silk inner robe: 121 x 186cm.
Hoosoo (Embroidered insignia)
: 70 x 26cm.
Horn girdle L. 130cm.
Ivory tablet 31.5 x 5cm.
1850.
Important Folklore Property No. 2 (designated in 1964).
Yi Royal Family Coll.
Duksoo Palace Museum, Seoul.

Ivory tablet

in the front and back, a *hoosoo* (embroidered insignia), a *dae* (girdle), a *geum-gwan* (black hat with gilt and gold stripes, denoting the rank by the number of the stripes), and a pair of low-sided, black, deer skin shoes. Two long pendants with jade and other beads were worn at both sides of the waist, and a tablet held in both hands completed the attire.

The red, wide sleeved outer and blue inner robes were unlined, made of line-patterned silk gauze, *hang-ra*, and bordered with a wide, black band at the broad collar, sleeve cuffs, and the hem, and had a *dongjuhng* (white neck band). The robe was fastened by *goreum* at the wearer's right side, and was secured internally by left-fastening smaller ties. A thin, white piping separated the black trimming from red silk. In the same material a blue silk, inner robe was flared from the armpit and was about 30 centimeters longer than the red, outer robe.

The two aprons with pleats were made of the same material as the outer robe, and were worn at the waist between the red and blue robes, so as to hang down in the front and back, slightly lower than the hem of the red robe. The aprons were attached by white or red knotted buttons through loops at the waist.

Another insignia of office, a *hoosoo* (back apron) of embroidered cranes with outstretched wings among stylized clouds, was composed of two vertical rows of white, blue, and yellow cranes on a red silk background, held by a band of white silk with black edges which was attached to side panels of blue silk at the waist. The cranes strained upward amidst clouds and were bordered above and below by two panels of embroidery. The upper border was composed of linked ovals encircling fylfot (*man-ja*), and a top row of colored stylized clouds on which a pair of large gold rings

Front view of *jobok*, Ewha Womans Univ. Museum, Seoul

Back view of *jobok*

were sewn for further embellishment. The lower border was composed of a row of linked ovals and a flower motif.

Jyebok : Mourning attire for Officials

Jyebok (mourning attire) was worn by civil and military officials when the king held memorial services for the royal ancestors and guardian deities of the State of the Yi Dynasty at the *Jongmyo* (Royal Ancestral Shrine). The robe was made of black silk gauze, had a round collar showing the white neck band of the inner robe, had large sleeves, and opened at both sides from the armpit and back at the high waist. It was bordered with the same black material around the neck line, hem and sleeve cuffs, was accented with very narrow, white piping, and fastened with a black *goreum*. The robe was worn over a white silk *joong-dan* (inner robe) which was longer, flared to the hem from the armpit, bordered as the outer robe, and fastened with black *goreum*.

With this robe, a *jye-gwan* (mourning cap), a *bang-shim-gokryong* (ritual token attached to the round collar), red skirt, *dae* (girdle), *hol* (tablet), red *pyeseul* (apron) between the inner and outer robe, a *hoosoo* (back apron with embroidery and tassels), leggings, white Korean cotton socks, and a pair of *hye* (low-sided shoes), were worn.

The *jye-gwan*, worn with *jyebok* (mourning attire) for the memorial services was made of rattan, covered with black gauze and the number of gold stripes denoting the rank of the wearer. The hair pin (jade, gold, silver, or wood) worn by officials was the same shape as the *geum-gwan*, which was brilliantly decorated with gold, but with less gilt decorations to show reverence, and had purple tassels at both ends of purple silk strings which went around the large pin on both sides.

Jyebok (black silk mourning attire)./ 19th c. / Suk Joo-sun Folk Art Museum, Seoul

81

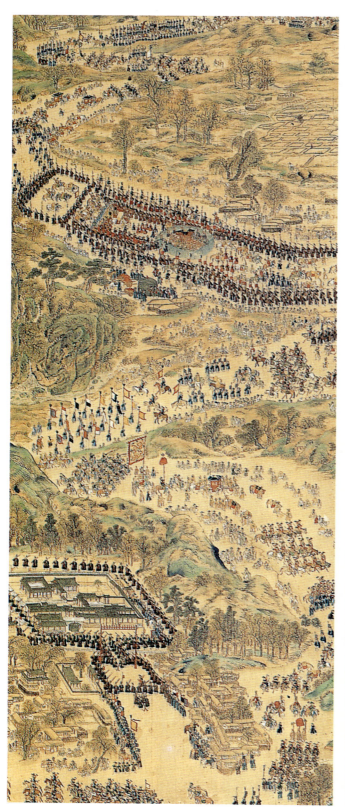

Back view of *jyebok*

Royal Procession to the King Jungjo's. Tomb.
214.5 x 73.5 cm. / 18th c.
Painting by Danwon, Kim Hong-do.
National Museum, Seoul

A travelogue published by an English writer, Mrs. Isabella Bird Bishop, in the 1890s, provides interesting information and details of the clothing of Koreans at that time:

> "Korean men wore white cotton-sleeved robes, huge trousers and socks; all wadded. They wore black, silk, wadded hats with pendants, sides edged with black fur, and rather high-crowned, broad-rimmed hats of black crinoline ribbon".

She also witnessed the procession of King Gojong (1863-1907) to the Royal Ancestral Shrine in 1897 or 1895:

> "Palace attendants in hundreds in brown glazed cotton sleeved cloaks, blue under robes tied below the knees with bunches of red ribbon, and stiff black hats, with heavy fan-shaped plumes of peacock's feathers, rode ragged ponies on gay saddles of great height...[High officials passed], superbly dressed... They wore black, highcrowned hats, with long crimson tassels behind, and front, mazarine blue silk robes, split up to the waist behind, with orange silk under robes and most voluminous crimson trousers, loosely tied above the ankles with knots of sky-blue ribbon, while streamers of ribbon fell from throats and girdles, and the hats were secured by throat sashes of large amber beads... sleeves were orange in the upper part and crimson in the lower, and very full."

❶ *Jye-gwan* (mourning hat) made of black silk gauze with gold stripes and gilt. / H. 22.5cm.
❷ *Hoosoo* (back apron)
❸ *Jye-hye* (black felt covered mourning shoes)
  Suk Joo-sun Museum, Seoul

Whole attire of *jyebok*

Shim-ui : Robes worn by scholars

During the Yi Dynasty, when Confucian scholarship was highly respected, only the most distinguished senior scholars were qualified to wear white robes with wide, black bands. Robes worn by scholars taking the civil service examinations, before becoming officials, were made of pale blue or pale green with wide bands of black. There were slight differences in style between the two kinds of robes worn by scholars and retired officials, the *hakchang-ui* and the *shim-ui*.

The *shim-ui* (white, wide sleeved robe) was silk for winter, cotton for spring and fall, and unlined *mosi* (fine ramie) for summer. It was trimmed with a wide, black border at the sleeve cuffs, neck opening, and along the hem line. It did not have the *dongjuhng* (white neck band), which has a philosophical meaning of respect and devotion for one's parents. The lower part of the high-waisted robe was made up of 12 panels, representing the 12 months of the year. The white chest band, trimmed in black, was tied by a black, braided, silk cord with tassels around the chest. Also with this robe, a black *bokkuhn* (hood of stiffened silk gauze), and *nokpihye* (deer skin boots) or *heukhye* (black felt boots decorated in white on the toes and heels) were worn. The whole attire resembled the coloring of the *hak* (crane) which symbolizes nobility, purity and sublimity.

Shim-ui (senior scholar's 12 panel robe of *sa*).
120 x 180cm. / 19th c.
Yi Royal Family coll.

The *hakchang-ui* (crane robe of the scholar), a less elaborate version worn by scholars for formal wear, included an elegant outer robe with wide sleeves, a slit opening in back from a high-waist, and a short slit on both sides. It flared from the armpit, was made of silk, cotton, *sa* or ramie, depending on the season, had *goreum*, and tied at the chest with black braided silk cords which had beads and tassels at the ends.

Sometimes the same style robe was also made in light blue to function as an inner robe for official occasions. White cloth shoes decorated in black and a black, high, square topped hat (one of the tiered hats), made of horse hair, completed the every day apparel of the Confucian aristocratic scholars in the Yi Dynasty.

Hakchang-ui (scholar's formal wear of *sa*).
120 x 180cm. / 18th c. / Suk Joo-sun Museum, Seoul

Dopo : Scholar's street wear

The *dopo*, in white or pale blue, was worn by men of letters and Confucian scholars. It was abolished in 1883 by a royal decree simplifying national costumes, but re-appeared after the seven year war with the Japanese (1892-1898), which was known as *Imjinwae-ran*. It was the common garment worn by public officials, noblemen, or commoners, in white for ordinary use and in light blue for festive occasions. It had wide sleeves with a small opening at the cuffs, a flared bottom, and an extra over-flap which was slit open, and was fastened by *goreum* and tied with a red, long, braided, silk cord with tassels at the chest for high ranking officials and blue or green for others. It was made of silk or cotton for winter, and ramie or *sa* for summer. A pair of leggings, white cotton socks and *heuk-hye* were worn by all ranks of officials.

Gaht & dopo

Dopo (ramie robe) for summer.
117 x 160cm.

Tasseled cord.
L. 396cm.
18th c.
Suk Joo-sun Museum, Seoul

Joongchimak & juhnbok : Scholar's casual wear

The *joongchimak* and *juhnbok* were a two piece ensemble worn for informal or leisure activities. The *joongchimak* was worn under a sleeveless outer coat, called *juhnbok*. The unlined *juhnbok*, which was influenced by a Chinese coat, had no sleeves and collar, and was used as a uniform for military officers until the end of the Yi Dynasty when King Gojong proclaimed the 'Costume Regulation Reform' in 1883. After 1888 the *juhnbok* became everyday apparel for civil and military officers. The *juhnbok* was made of patterned, silk gauze in various colors, was joined on top by a tiny sash, and opened all the way down to the hem. The back was opened from the high waist to the ankle-length hem and both sides were also slit open a little at the bottom for better mobility. It tied at the chest with a long, braided, red silk cord with tassels (*sedodae*). With this robe, scholars wore *bokkuhn*, leggings, and *chohye* (straw sandals) or *heukhye*.

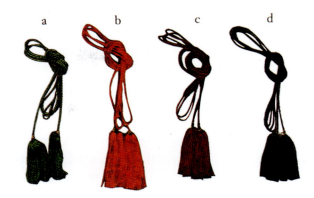

Tasseled cord for man's outer robe.
L. a. 382cm, b. 394cm, c. 400cm, d. 328cm.
19th c.
Suk Joo-sun Museum, Seoul

Gaht : Hat made of horse hair)

Hats and headdress were an essential part of the dress code throughout Korean costume history. From the unique, dazzling, gold crowns of the Shilla Kings to the wide-brimmed, black, horsehair hat of noblemen of the Yi Dynasty, all headdress signified social position and profession.

The kings wore *geum-gwan* (gold crowns) for official functions. The courtiers wore *samo* (caps with side-flaps). Scholars wore *sabang-gwan* (square hats), *jungja-gwan* (three tiered hats) or *tang-guhn* (hats worn only inside the house, made of horsehair over a bamboo frame). Even the farmers, Buddhist monks, and other low class professionals were identified by their hats.

Traditionally, unmarried men continued to have ponytails or single braids (queues or plaits), tied with string, hanging down their backs, until they were married. Later, during the Three Kingdoms Period, their hair was trimmed, bound in a knot on the top of their heads (*sangtu*), and worn with a *gaht*. Under the *gaht*, a small, black, rimless, horsehair beanie actually covered the *sangtu*.

Joongchimak (sky-blue ramie robe). / 102 x 150cm.
Juhnbok (indigo blue *sa* sleeveless robe) / L. 115cm.

Around the forehead a *mangguhn* (horsehair headband) was worn to secure the *gaht* on the head. On an ancient mural in the Koguryo tomb (Gamshin-chong), the men's top-knot looks very similar but much larger than the top-knot worn during the Yi Dynasty.

When Confucianism began to dominate Korean society from the end of the 14th century, the *gaht*, one of the most unique hats in the world, became an important item for the proper attire of Korean men. In the 15th century, men's clothing was standardized. Thus, until fashion was liberalized in 1895, lower class men were not allowed to wear the *gaht*. The *gaht*, woven in a loose and airy gauze, was firm and straight, not hard like steel, but made of the soft hair of a horse's tail. It was the lightest among the hats known to us. It neither protected from the rain, sun, wind, or cold, and was so transparent that it showed the top-knot and the horsehair headband worn under it. Very fine hair-thin bamboo strands (or slivers) were also used for the top. The *gaht* made of straw for young men, was called *tcho-rip*, and was not transparent.

Tcho-rip (straw hat for young men)
19th c.
Suk Joo-sun Museum, Seoul

There were two kinds of *gaht*, fine and coarse, depending on the material used and the skill of the craftsmen. The top of the hat was woven with horsehair or very fine bamboo strands over a wooden form, and then boiled before it was removed from the form. After the brim was woven with horsehair, a mixture of glue and black ink was applied to hold it together firmly and to give resistance to wear and tear. The brim was then ironed to give it a slight inward curve. Finally, several layers of a glue and lacquer mixture were applied to the hat to make it stiff.

After the rule on hats was adopted in the early Yi Dynasty, shops were opened to produce horsehair hats under the management of the government. *Yangtae* shops produced the brims, and *moja* (hat) shops made the top part of the hats out of horsehair. *Mangguhn* shops made the horsehair headbands. *Mogyong* shops made hat strings, which were more for ornamentation than for fastening the hat. All parts of the hat were

Gold Crown (*geum-gwan* for officials).
H. 22 cm / Dia. 20 x 15 cm
Yi Dynasty
Suk Joo-sun Museum, Seoul

Tang-guhn made of horsehair, worn only inside the house.

then assembled by craftsmen who also repaired old hats.

Over the centuries the basic style of the *gaht*, the flat top and wide brimmed hat, changed little. The exception was during the early part of the Yi Dynasty when very broad brims (from 60 to 70 cm.) were more popular than the narrower ones (30cm.) worn in the later part of the Yi Dynasty (20th century). It is said that the wide brimmed *gaht*s, worn by civil and military officials above the 3rd rank, prevented them from whispering to each other during audiences. *Gaht*s were worn by men when they went out or received guests at home. The *gaht* might have been worn inside the home as well as on the streets.

The *gaht* was stored in a hat-box when not in use. Elaborate hat-boxes were handsomely designed in different shapes out of thin wood of paulownia and paper. Octagonal shaped hat-boxes were made by pasting mulberry paper in layers, varnished, and then decorated with auspicious symbols. Special containers were made for the *mangguhn* also. *Galmo* (cone shaped, oiled, paper hats) were used as a cover over the *gaht* in the rain.

※ There is record that one king, over two thousand years ago, decreed a law that all men should wear ceramic hats. If the man's ceramic hat did not have any chips or breaks, he was considered to be most even tempered and had a good chance of getting a government position.

Taesahye : Silk covered leather shoes

Taesahye for *yangban* men and boys, (slippers made of layers of paper or cotton and leather), were covered with green, silk damask and applique at the toes and heels in red, silk damask.

Even the king wore this with his informal everyday wear. White linear patterns also decorated the toes and heels. This low-sided silk shoe was lined with either leather or silk, had flat soles with round-headed metal nails, and was either black or white.

Gaht (*Heuk-rip*, man's wide brimmed hat).
Black horsehair.
H. 13.5cm.
19th c.
Suk Joo-sun Museum, Seoul

Taesahye (upper class man's silk shoes) for men.
Green silk damask.
L. 27cm.

89

heuk-hye

Green silk damask *taesahye* for boy.
L. 15cm.

Taesahyes & Got-shins / 20th c.

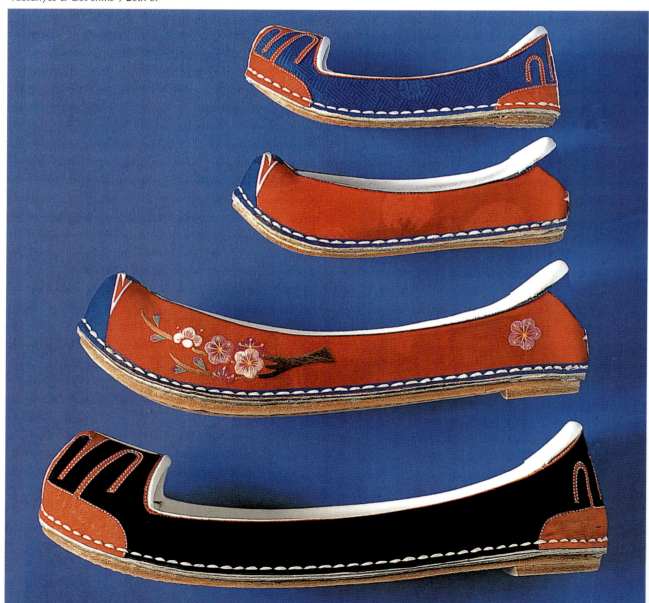

Heuk-hwa (black, mid-calf length, leather or felt boots with red trimming), *heuk-hye* (black, low-sided, leather or felt shoes), *mok-hwa* (felt boots also with red trimming), and *gajook-mituri* (leather-sandals) were worn with *gwan-bok* (uniforms) by officials.

Buhsuhn : Korean white cotton socks

Hanbok wearers, men and women of all ages, wore *buhsuhn* indoors. Over the *buhsuhn* they would slip on their shoes when they went outside. However, outdoor shoes were always taken off before entering a room.

Buhsuhn, a plain, white, cotton sock, which was unlined in the summer, lined for spring and fall, and lined and padded with thin layers of cotton batting in the winter, were worn by people of all ages and sex. These cotton socks with upturned toes formed ankles, like a boot, and had round heels. They are still worn by *hanbok* wearers of today. For a Korean woman to have an egg-shaped heel was considered the essence of loveliness. And, it was said that the prettiest foot was shaped like a cucumber seed. Thus, Koreans turned the most abused part of the body, the foot, into a thing of beauty by wearing the *buhsuhn* which achieved this distinction. The *buhsuhn* was the only part of Korean clothing that fit exactly. It did not come off easily once it was on, but retained its beautiful form even after it was taken off, unlike the western style stocking which lays limply when taken off. So beautiful is the *buhsuhn* that it can be used as a decoration!

Small, baby *buhsuhn* lined, padded, quilted, and embroidered with colorful plum flowers had red silk tassels on the upturned toes, and red ribbons around the ankles to keep them in place. They were worn by a baby on the first birthday or on holidays.

Buhsuhn pattern holders, small, red silk envelopes in the shape of square hot-pot holders, contained the *buhsuhn* patterns of all of the family members. These patterns, made of rice paper, were folded and stored

Adult's *buhsuhn*

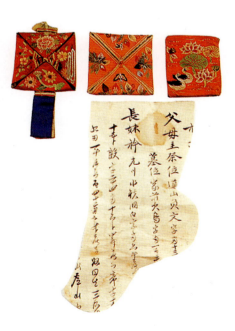

Pattern (made of mulberry paper) & pattern holder

carefully inside. The pattern holders had openings at the corners, a loop for hanging, and were usually embroidered with a pair of cranes surrounded by other floral designs, a symbol of a happy marriage.

Buhsuhn-jang (small chests) to keep the *buhsuhn* in by the dozens, were indispensable furniture items for any woman in a Korean house.

Children's *buhsuhn* (cotton with embroidery)

Hyoongbae : Emblematic square badges for officials

The first discussion about the use of *hyoongbae* (square badges) was brought up in 1446 at King Sejong's court. Some of the court members were against the idea, since the austere Confucian government supposedly encouraged frugality and the restraint of luxury. The *dae* (girdle) was already in use to identify the ranks by jade, gold, silver, brass or buffalo-horn plaques. Eight years later, in June 1454, the subject of *hyoongbae* came up again.

This time the *hyoongbae* system was agreed upon and carried out with four divine animals to distinguish the ranks. The insignia system was simplified after the reign of King Soonjong. Twin cranes were for high ranking civil officials of 1st to 3rd rank, and a single crane for the lower rank of 4th to 9th rank. For military officers, twin tigers were used for the high 1st to 3rd rank, and a single tiger for the 4th to 9th rank. The right to wear the badges was bestowed by the emperor. The badges were made in one piece, then sewn to the robe so that they could be replaced if the wearer's rank

Children's *buhsuhn*

Hyoongbae of twin cranes embroidered with gold thread on blue, silk damask.
17.5 x 19.5cm. / 1780. / Suk Joo-sun Museum, Seoul

changed. The square badges, with designs of cranes flying with outstretched wings among various longevity symbols, or with roaring tigers, were attached on the chest and back of the robe.

For civil officials, the cranes dominated the design with outstretched wings. The position of the crane, straining upwards through stylized clouds, with long legs trailing below, and holding a piece of *Bullocho* (plant of a eternal youth) in their beaks, symbolized the loftiness of the spirit of a learned man, and high-minded integrity. The design was embroidered on patterned, silk satin or damask about 20cm. square in size. The whole square was basted with rice paper and lined. The rocks and waves were cleverly stitched for the best effect. The stylized waves were raised from the surface by couching tightly rolled pieces of paper onto the pattern before sewing over the top with thread. The feathers and outline of the cranes were also raised by thread padding formed by the stitches.

During the reign of King Gojong (1864-1896 A.D.), his father, the Regent Daewongoon, wore an insignia with a *kirin* (an imaginary animal) motif. But in 1895 he changed it to a turtle. The insignia for the king's relatives and sons-in-law were thickly embroidered with gold and silver threads to distinguish them from court officials.

The *hyoongbae* made in earlier periods were larger in size and the color of the threads were subdued, showing the fineness in the embroidery as compared to the later period *hyoongbae*. The commoners were allowed to use the *hyoongbae* only on the front and back of ceremonial robes for 60th birthdays, for wedding grooms, and children's 1st birthdays.

A square, dark blue, cloud-patterned, silk damask with two, white, roaring tigers surrounded by longevity symbols, was assigned to high ranking military officers. Between the two tigers, a small *taegeuk* (*yin/yang* symbol) represents the ancient Oriental philosophy of universal harmony, *yin* and *yang* (light and darkness). This accompanied the idea that the five primary elements; wood, metal, fire, water, and earth, which make up the universe through their various combinations, was part of the creation of all beings. It is believed that human beings must conform to the cosmic working of *yin-yang* and live in harmony with the five elements, maintaining a utopian balance and harmony.

A tiger was considered a wise animal which had great power for discipline, punished evil, and was faithful and loyal. Thus this tiger's imposing pose represented the warrior's brave spirit, discipline, and integrity.

Eventually, the use of the *hyoongbae* was abolished at the end of the Yi Dynasty in 1899. Thousands of pairs of rank badges depicting the cranes in flight have survived, although the motifs of rocks, clouds, waves and 'plant of eternal youth' continuously remained for 300 years. The designs appear in infinite variety.

※ Social status was set by the imperial government, the more educated group of respected civil scholar officials administered government, while the military officers were responsible for the internal stability and external defense of the country. There were nine ranks within the civil and military order.

Hyoongbae with twin crane.
Cranes embroidered with gold thread on indigo blue damask.
34.5 x 36.5 cm
1460.
Suk Joo-sun Museum, Seoul

Hyoongbae with Kirin (for the Regent Daewon-goon, Father of the King Gojong)
Embroidered with gold thread on black silk satin.
17.5 x 19 cm.
Yi Dynasty

Hyoongbae with single crane.
Crane embroidered with silver thread on blue silk damask.
18 x 19cm.
1650
Suk Joo-sun Museum, Seoul

Hyoongbae with twin tigers.
Tigers embroidered with white thread on blue silk damask.
25.5 x 28cm.
1720 / Suk Joo-sun Museum, Seoul

Official Dress for Women

Women of the Yi Dynasty court did not have social activities outside of their homes. From the young age of seven, women were secluded in the female quarters of the house, learning how to sew and embroider, and spending their days painting, weaving, and socializing among themselves. Meanwhile, an emperor or *yangban* was not limited in the number of wives and consorts he might have. Still, only one wife could be designated as the empress at any time. No men, except eunuchs, were allowed into the women's quarters, not even physicians. The finest embroidery work was done by these court ladies during the Yi Dynasty. There, in the 'Secret Garden' in the Changdok Palace, behind the 'Royal Library', was a building where court ladies raised silkworm cocoons and wove silk. It is still preserved, as is a hundred year old mulberry tree, whose leaves were used to feed the silkworms.

Dress of the Empress (or Queen)

Juhg-ui : Official Court Robe

Juhg-ui, the exquisite, shimmering, silk ceremonial robes for the Yi Dynasty queens, were adopted from Ming China, and worn from 1897 on during the reign of King Gojong (1863-1907). The *juhg-ui* was worn by the queen (or empress) as a sacerdotal robe (parallel to the king's *gujangbok*). It was also worn by the wife of the Crown Prince, and the eldest son, for state coronation ceremonies and court weddings. The wide sleeved, deep blue robe had 138 pairs of pheasants arranged in 12 rows with 160 small plum blossoms in between embroidered in brilliant silk threads of five colors and gold thread. Gold-leaf imprints were on the red silk borders all along the neckline, front opening, hemline, and sleeve cuffs in a dragon motif. The queen's emblematic medallions with five-clawed dragons (four-clawed dragons for the wife of the crown prince), embroidered with gold threads, were attached on the chest, back, and shoulders. *Juhg-ui* was worn over a trailing, long, red silk skirt with a blue border and a gold-leaf imprint of a phoenix and clouds. The length of the front was the same as the skirt worn underneath, but the back was 30cm. longer than the front.

The *pyeseul* (short, front, knee covers or aprons) with six pairs of pheasants and plum blossoms in between the pheasants,

Juhg-ui paper pattern.

Ttul-jam (jade hairpins with fluttering ornaments)
10.3 x 8.5 cm

Ttul-jam (small hair pin with fluttering butterfly design on a coiled gold wire with pearl, jade, sapphire, coral and ruby).
L. 9.8cm / 1860.
L. 10.3cm / 1860.
L. 9cm / 1860
Suk Joo-sun Museum, Seoul

Hwa-gwan (jeweled *jogdoori*)
Red silk covered ceremonial crown for the queen.
H. 9cm. / 1780.
H. 12cm / 1870.
Suk Joo-sun Museum, Seoul

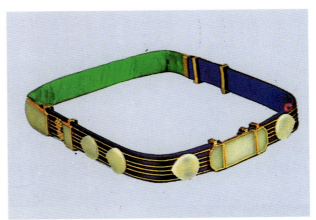

Empress' or queen's *Okdae*

Tchuhngsuk (blue silk covered shoes to match the *juhg-ui*).
Yi Dynasty
Suk Joo-sun Museum, Seoul

97

Dae-su worn by the queen and princess of *Yongchinwang* family.

were embroidered on the same material as the robe. The *pyeseul* was bordered with red brocade that was decorated with four dragons and cloud motifs in gold-leaf imprints, and worn over the great robe. The *hoo-seul* (back apron of 3 panels) with fringes at the end in red, green, blue, and white, was also worn at the back. A long *hapi* (stole) of the same material was lined with pink silk, had a single phoenix in flight, and a cloud motif in gold-leaf imprint. It was draped in the front, around the neck, and over both shoulders. *Juhg-ui* also could be made in red, and originally the 156 pairs of pheasants were woven with the addition of gold threads, instead of embroidered.

The queen wore *okdae* (a jade girdle) above *dae-dae* (large sash), and held a jade tablet. She wore a *juk-gwan* (queen's crown) or *dae-su* (enlarged coiffure with a wig), a *hwa-gwan* (ceremonial *jogdoori*), and a pair of blue socks and beautiful *tchuhngsuk* (blue silk covered leather shoes), for court attire.

Gachae (an elaborate wig) with two big, gold hair pins in phoenix designs, a large gold *binyuh* (crossbar) decorated with enamel and semi-precious gems at one end, two large hair pins decorated with precious stones, a smaller gold crossbar below the headband and above the forehead, a very large gold crossbar with a phoenix (*bong-jam*) at the end, a big jade pin at the top of the wig, and a *daenggi* for the chignon, were all worn with *juhg-ui*.

Tchuhngsuk : Blue silk ceremonial shoes

Indigo blue silk shoes, decorated with clouds and dragon motif applique and beads on the toes, were worn by the empress with her ceremonial robe toward the end of the Yi Dynasty.

i (Queen's great ceremonial robe) with 312 pheasants in 12 rows. / 155 x 56.5 cm.

The same style of shoes were worn by the wife of the Crown Prince, but with a design of clouds and phoenixes.

Wonsam : Minor ceremonial robe

The *nok-wonsam* (green ceremonial robe) was worn by the princesses and queen consort at minor ceremonies. High ranking court ladies and nobility wore this at major ceremonies. From the end of the Yi Dynasty, the commoners were allowed to wear the *nok-wonsam* for wedding ceremonies only once in their life time, but in simpler versions. The *nok-wonsam* was made of silk satin or brocade in the winter, lined with red silk, and bordered in blue at the hem. In the summer, it was made of *hwamunsa* (stiffened, flower patterned, silk gauze). The robe was held at the end of the collar by knotted buttons, and worn over the yellow *juhgori* and two skirts. The front panel was 30cm. shorter than the back to reveal the red skirt, which was shorter than the blue inner skirt. Both sides were open from the armpits and at the front center. The front and back were each 44cm. wide, and looked more like panels over the voluminous skirts. The robe was embellished with gold-leaf imprints of the Chinese characters of *bok* (good luck)

Nok-wonsam worn by Princess Duhgon (1822-1844), the 3rd daughter of King Sunjo (1790-1834) when she was 16 years old, and married to Yun Ui-son.
It was destroyed during the Korean War in 1950.
Gold-leaf imprints of stylized *su* were embellished profusely all over the robe.
164 x 328cm.
19th c.
Important Folklore Property No. 211.
Suk Joo-sun Museum, Seoul

Wonsam (green silk brocade robe)
It is closed by two silver buttons in bat shape with cloisonne and pear flower (royal family crest).

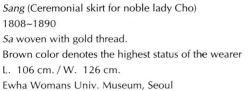

Sang (Ceremonial skirt for noble lady Cho)
1808~1890
Sa woven with gold thread.
Brown color denotes the highest status of the wearer
L. 106 cm. / W. 126 cm.
Ewha Womans Univ. Museum, Seoul

and/or *su* (long life) and flowers with scrolling vines. It had large sleeves with *saektong* (wide stripes of red, yellow and/or blue), and *hansam* (long, white, unlined, tube-like cloth) attached at the ends and draped over the wearer's hands. A wide, long, red chest band with gold-leaf imprints was tied at the back. Also worn was an enlarged coiffure, a *gachae* (wig), a pair of white cotton socks, and *danghye* (silk covered, leather shoes).

Lady Yang

Nok-wonsam (Bridal robe)
Gap-sa woven with clouds and bat motif.
L. 131.4 cm.
W. of sleeves. 88 cm.
Ewha Womans Univ. Museum.

※ Oiled paper covered the collar for preservation.

Royal concubine Lady Yang wearing *wonsam*.
Suk Joo-sun Memorial Museum.

Danghye : Silk covered leather shoes for women

Danghye, flat heeled leather shoes, covered the top of stiffened layers of stitched cotton with silk damask. Sometimes pretty flower designs were embroidered. They were hand-sewn and hand cushioned with layers of cotton pads for leather soles, appliqued at the turned-up toes and heels with different colored silk damask in stylized patterns, and stitched along the sole line with matching colored threads. Inside they were lined with white leather. *Danghye* were usually worn by queens and wives of the Crown Prince for auspicious ceremonies at court such as state weddings or enthronements. Later at the end of the Yi Dynasty, the commoners were allowed to wear *danghye*, and it became a part of proper attire. *Danghye* is also called *mareun-shin* (dry shoes) or flower shoes. *Yoohye* (or *jin-shin*, oiled shoes) were worn on rainy days.

Danghye with embroidery and applique on toes and heels
Suk Joo-sun Museum, Seoul

Dang-ui : Minor ceremonial jacket

Dang-ui (semi-formal ceremonial jackets) were mainly worn by the Empress (yellow),

Dang-ui worn by Princess Duhgon, 3rd daughter of King Sunjo.
Patterned silk brocade with gold-leaf imprints in *su* and *bok*.
130 x 75cm.
1837
Important Folklore Material No. 1
Suk Joo-sun Museum, Seoul

the Queen (purplish red), the Crown Prince's wife and princesses (green), high ranking court ladies and royal concubines for minor ceremonies, and by noble women for major ceremonies.

The jacket was characterized by simple styling and elongated panels in the front and back in a semilunar shaped hem. It was curved smoothly from the armpit.

The *dang-ui* was made of silk brocade woven in dragon, phoenix, flower or Chinese character motifs and lined with red or purple silk for the winter, and *sa* for the summer. It was fastened with dark red *goreum* at the right side of the chest and a smaller inner *goreum* was tied at the left inside. It was trimmed in white at the sleeve cuffs and collar.

The white sleeve bands were attached only to ceremonial jackets. The length of the jacket was 80cm. (about 3 times longer than the *juhgori*), and was sometimes embellished all over with gold-leaf imprints in Chinese characters of *su* and *bok*. To indicate their rank, *bo* (embroidered emblematic medallions) were attached on the front, back, and shoulders. The dark blue, silk skirt was embellished with gold-leaf imprints of clouds and phoenix motifs in two wide rows. The chignon was decorated with red *daenggi*, fastened by one *binyuh*, and worn with a *chilbo-hwagwan* (seven-jeweled crown). *Buhsuhn* and yellow silk covered shoes completed the attire.

Yellow *sa dang-ui* with Chinese character motif.

Summer *dang-ui* worn by court ladies.
The material was so thin that a hem would have been visible.
So, the end thread was pulled, gathering the edges inward.
Ewha Womans Univ. Museum

Plain Clothes of the Queen

The queen wore indigo blue silk skirts and *samhoejang juhgori* in different designs from the clothes worn by court ladies. The *tchung-sam* (green jacket) worn by Queen Gwanghaegun (1576-1623), was made of a dark green flower and bird-patterned silk brocade. It was long in length and sleeves, had a wide collar, and a very short and narrow *goreum*.

There were ten Chinese characters of longevity for the queen written inside the white neckband of the jacket.

Queen Gwanghaegoon's silk brocade *juhgori* (1576-1623). Suk Joo-sun Memorial Folk Art Museum, Seoul.

Hwal-ot : Bridal robe for *Pyebaek* ceremony

Noble women's bridal robes, *hwal-ot*, were worn by the princesses and daughters of the nobility of the Yi Dynasty for weddings and during the memorial rites of the bridegroom's ancestors after the wedding ceremony.

The red silk satin robe had a purple lining, long back and short front panels, and an opening at the center and both sides from armpit. Elaborate, rich embroideries on the two front panels, a seamless back panel (train), sleeves, and both shoulders of red silk satin, made the *hwal-ot* a brilliant, sumptuous, ceremonial garment. The long sleeves were accentuated by *saektong*, broad bands of yellow, blue, and red, ending with an even broader, embroidered, full, white sleeves. The panels were filled with auspicious symbols, compositions of lotus and peony flowers and leaves, stylized waves and rocks called 'isles of immortals in the sea of longevity' (*su-san-bok-hae*), peach plants in pots, a pair of small birds, butterflies, and a pair of large cranes. The sleeves were embroided with lotus, peony, and chrysanthemum flowers and leaves, birds, butterflies, waves, rocks, peacocks, and phoenixes, symbolizing the hope for a long and happy marriage. The robe was in the same shape as *wonsam*.

The crimson red, silk satin *hwal-ot* was worn over a traditional bridal green silk *juhgori* and a long, trailing, red silk *chima* embellished with a broad band of gold-leaf imprints of auspicious characters and motifs. *Hwal-ot* were fastened around the chest by *bong-dae*, a 350cm-long, folded, red, satin cloth with a phoenix motif, gold-leaf imprinted chest band, at the back. At the end of the back panel, two small loops were attached to make it easy to handle by two helping ladies during the bowing procedure. The bride wore a *hwa-gwan* (jeweled *jugdoori*), a pair of white *buhsuhn* and embroidered silk shoes.

Immediately following the wedding ceremony, the bride performed a formal introduction-bowing ceremony to her parents-in-law and other close relatives

(called *pyebaek*). The help of two ladies, one on each side, was needed, since deep bowing began from a standing position with both hands covered by a *hansam* (plain, white, long, light-weight silk) and held up to the forehead. Then she had to slowly sit down to the floor, bending her body so that her hands and head almost touched the floor, and stand up again to repeat the process.

Reproduction of *hwal-ot.* / 20th c.

Hwal-ot (princess' bridal robe).
Red light-weight wool.
121 x 138cm.
1680.
Suk Joo-sun Folk Art Museum

Hwal-ot reproduction of the princess Bog-on, 2nd daughter of King Sunjo (1801-1834) in 1983
Changdok Palace Museum, Seoul

Back view of *hwal-ot* and *doturak-daenggi*

Back view of the princess Bog-on's *hwal-ot* reproduction

Doturak-daenggi : Ceremonial hair ribbon

Large, wide, black, silk ribbons called *doturak-daenggi* were used by young, upper-class women for ceremonial occasions. They were doubled and decorated with brooch-like scalloped, white jade, coral, and red silk threads. They were further embellished with round cloisonné and two large rosette-shaped, silk tassels, and imprinted gold-leaf in designs of flowers, birds, and stylized characters. The ribbons hung from the nape of the neck over the chignon, and down the back, and over the outer robe.

Ceremonial hair ribbons for upper class, young women were embroidered and decorated with floral cloisonné and red,

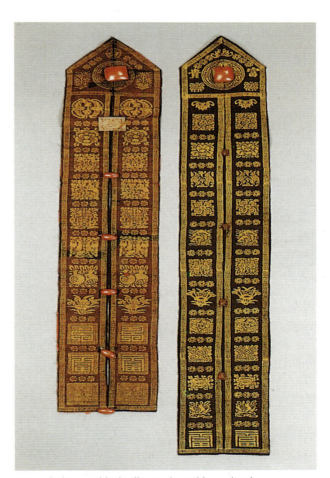

Doturak-daenggi.(black silk satin hair ribbon) / 19th c.

109

long, silk tassels fastened by silver bands at intervals along the border of a black background. The *doturak-daenggi* was allowed to be worn by commoners for the traditional wedding ceremony. A smaller one with gold-leaf imprints which draped over both ends of the crossbar hung in front, and a large one was worn on the back.

The *daenggi* (hair ribbon) for the pigtails of a young boy was made of silk, and was sometimes embroidered in a satin stitch or gold-leaf imprints. The gold-leaf imprint, with 6 auspicious characters (longevity, wealth, nobility, many male sons) on a black silk ribbon, was used by a royal prince of the Yi Dynasty.

● *Geum-bak-pan* : Pattern board for gold-and silver-leaf imprint

It is not known exactly when gold-leaf imprints were first used to embellish garments in Korea.

Although an impressive variety of gold accessories were found in the royal tombs of the Shilla Kingdom, and gold powder was widely used in Buddhist paintings during the Koryo Dynasty, most of the existing Yi Dynasty royal costumes decorated with gold-leaf imprints are dated to the later part of the dynasty.

Only royal family members' ceremonial clothing was embellished with gold-leaf imprints. The queens' robes were imprinted with dragon motifs while the princesses' were imprinted with phoenix and flower motifs, symbolizing the supreme power of the ruling family. Therefore, it was unthinkable for commoners to decorate their clothing with gold-leaf, even if they could afford to do so, during the Yi Dynasty. With Japan's annexation of Korea in 1910, and the fall of Korea's last monarchy, many societal customs changed and the class system was abolished. Therefore, as clothing was no longer exclusively a royal status symbol, traditional gold-leaf imprint came to be used by everyone.

Gold-leaf imprinting, like any other traditional handicraft, took many years of training to master. Kim Dok-hwan, son of the master of Korean traditional arts and crafts, Kim Kyong-yong, designated as a 'Intangible Cultural Asset' by the government, carries on his father's prized skill with the help of his wife, Lee Chong-ja, in Bundang-gu, Sungnam-shi, Kyounggi-do. Recently, his college educated son, Ki-ho and daughter, In-shin decided to follow their father's profession.

There are four stages for imprinting gold-leaf on garments in the traditional Korean way: carving patterns on woodblocks, preparing the gold-leaf, making the glue, and then stamping. Pattern boards were used to imprint gold or silver leaf imprints onto clothes. They were usually made of the wood of fine-grained, hard, pear trees, ginkgo trees, or birchwood, which were all supple enough for carving yet durable. The wood was cut into an appropriate size, planed smoothly, and polished with sandpaper before carving.

Then, a desired pattern was drawn with a brush and ink on mulberry paper. Next, the paper was pasted onto the smooth surface of the woodblock with glue made of rice. Carving was done with great care to preserve all of the fine and delicate lines. About 20 different kinds of carving knives were used for over 700 different designs, including Chinese characters for such things as longevity, happiness and successful rule, and flowers, animals, birds, and fruits.

110

After carving, the surface of the woodblock was polished again with sandpaper. Then it was boiled in water mixed with vegetable oil, and touched up again with sandpaper before drying in the shade.

Preparing the gold-leaf required the greatest skill and labor. A piece of pure gold, (usually about 45 grams), was placed on an anvil, made into a thin plate by hammering with a tin hammer for about three days and nights, and cut into small, square pieces about 2 × 2 cm.

Costume by Huh-young & gold-leaf imprinted by Kim Dok-hwan

111

Each piece was wrapped with mulberry paper, coated with lacquer, and wrapped again with thick paper. Then, it was hammered for three more days and nights. After this hammering process, the gold plates had turned into leaves thinner than the thinnest paper that would blow away by one's breath. Each leaf was moved with a pincer onto a small, square piece of mulberry paper, and was ready for stamping.

The glue for silk clothing was made from fish bladders. The bladders were boiled in a mixture of water and vegetable oil over medium heat all day. (A little amount of honey added to the glue slowed down the hardening speed in the winter). The glue was applied to the carved woodblock with a brush, or a roller for better speed and eveness, and warmed over heat a few times between brushings. Then the wood-block was placed in the desired position for imprinting, pressed with both hands, and removed quickly. The gold leaves were afixed to the clothes by stroking them with the fingers quickly and repeatedly with great care. The most important part of the whole process was not breathing and not keeping the windows open, even in the hot summer. Today, air conditioners and fake gold make artisan's work easier, and gold or silver-imprints are widely used by all for wedding ceremonial dresses, children's clothes, hair ribbons, pouches, and more.

Headdress for the Upper class Women

Nuhwool : Framed veils

Nuhwool were a head garment worn only by upper class women of the Yi Dynasty. Wide, long, ground level, silk material, mostly in black or dark blue, was attached to a round hat, and covered the whole body, head to toe. It became a part of upper class women's proper attire when going outside. A queen of the Yi Dynasty would wear dignified *nuhwool*, lined with the same material, but unlined in the front in order to be able to see through it. They wore purple silk *nuhwool* with red silk sashes when visiting

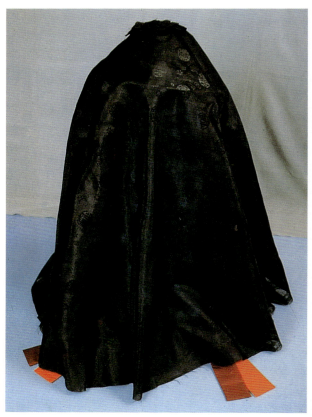

Nuhwool of purple silk *sa*. / Suk Joo-sun Museum, Seoul

Shorter *nuhwool* was worn ordinarily.

the royal tombs or during royal processions. Loosely woven, see-through, thin material was used for the part that covered the face, allowing them a hazy view. Shorter versions of the *nuhwool* were worn by lower ranking ladies when they went out.

Therefore, the world that upper class women of the Yi Dynasty saw was always hazy and misty, as if seen through a fog.

Jogdoori : Jeweled crown

The custom of aristocratic ladies wearing the *jogdoori* began from the Koryo period (918-1392). According to the *Koryo-sa* (History of Koryo), the Yuan Chinese (1279-1368) sent *kokori* (*gwan* or crown) to the queen of the Koryo Kingdom as a gift. Archeologists determined that the word *kokori* (*gwan* or crown) changed to *jogdoori* along the way. Choi Nam-sun (a scholar, Yuk-dang, 1890-1957), stated in his book, *Kosatong* (Ancient History) that the *jogdoori* was a Mongolian fashion, which Mongolian women wore when they went out. But the Koryo noble ladies wore it as a part of the ceremonial costume. It is believed, by some, that people began to use *jogdoori* from King Moonmu (661-681 B.C.) of the Shilla Kingdom's period.

According to the *Imhasilgi* record, from the time of King Gwanghaegun (1608-1623), *jogdoori* made of unbleached cotton on the outside and lined with reddish maroon was worn. It was so popular that it became a national custom to wear one. This proves that *jogdoori* has been worn even before the *gachae* prohibition.

During the Yi Dynasty, aristocratic ladies began to wear big *gachae* (wigs) with various kinds of lavish decorations such as semi-precious stones, pearls, and coral. These decorations became extravagant and outrageously expensive. King Yongjo (1724-1776) proclaimed a sumptuary law in 1756 (year 21) prohibiting the wearing of *gachae*.

Instead, the king ordered them to wear *jogdoori*. Thus, this simple style was especially encouraged for the general populace after the prohibition order of 1781 was declared. The *jogdoori* worn by the queens and noble ladies of the Yi Dynasty, was called *hwa-gwan* (jeweled *jogdoori*), and worn with their ceremonial robes such as the *hwal-ot, juhg-ui, wonsam,* and *dang-ui*.

The *hwa-gwan* was colorfully decorated with lavish, expensive jewels. The *hwa-gwan*, in the shape of a small pillbox hat, was made of multi-layered black silk. Simple in shape, this crown was decorated with gold-leaf butterfly shapes attached by gold, spring-like, wire coils, which fluttered with slight movements. The crown was embellished with jade, pearls, coral, quartz, amethysts, turquoise, amber (symbol of Buddha's mercy), and silk tassels. Two silk ribbons were attached on each side for tying behind the ears under the chignon. As these crowns became more extravagant, there was another sumptuary law in 1781, prohibiting even renting or loaning the *hwa-gwan* (seven-jeweled *jogdoori)* for wedding ceremonies, which was a custom allowed for commoners once in their life time. However, the custom of wearing pretty *jogdoori* continues as part of the traditional wedding attire for the bride, and for little girls at their first birthday celebration.

Nambawi : Silk hooded winter hat

The *nambawi* probably has the longest history among the winter hats. In the beginning, only men and women of the upper class wore it. Later it was worn by the commoners, and still later the *nambawi* was

113

jogdoori.
H. 7.5 cm / 1880s
H. 6 cm / 1880s
Suk Joo-sun Museum, Seoul

Jobawi
H. 20cm / 1900s

Nambawi (winter hat with long back flap)
Black silk satin or brocade.
L. 42cm.
19th c.
Oryudae Memorial Museum of Korean Martyrs, Seoul

Jobawi (young women's winter hat).
Red silk brocade.
L. 26cm.
19th c.
Oryudae Memorial Museum of Korean Martyrs, Seoul

worn only by women. This black silk brocade or satin hat was lined with soft cotton or flannel in green, blue, and purple, or lined with fur, padded, and bordered with fur. It had a round opening at the top and covered the head, forehead, and ears with red flaps, and the back of the neck by a long, back flap. Red silk sashes, attached to the ear-flaps, were tied under the chin to hold the hat covering the ears. Gold-leaf imprints in various symbols of Chinese characters (longevity, happiness, wealth, nobility, many sons) with flower and bird motifs along the borders, embellished the hat.

Jobawi : Silk women's winter hat

The close-fitting women's hat, *jobawi*, also had round openings at the top and covered the head, forehead, and ears, but not the braid or the chignon in the back. It originated from an ear-covering, and was restyled for women from the men's hat. The *jobawi* was made of black or purple, silk satin or brocade, lined with blue or brown silk or soft cotton, and decorated with small, carved, jade disks at the front and back with silk tassels. A single string of coral beads looped on one side to link the front and back tassels, and gold or silver-leaf imprints along the border. During the end of the Yi Dynasty, the *jobawi* became very popular and women of all classes wore it when they went out.

Jangshingu (accessories)

The history of accessories in Korea goes way back to the prehistoric age, when beads (stone and shell bits) were used as ornaments and for earrings and necklaces in the Mahan period (2nd-1st century B.C.).

Samjak norigae
Silver with cloisonné.
L. 10cm.
19th c.
The Chang Sook-hwan collection.

Highly sophisticated precious metal (gold and silver) ornaments of the Shilla, such as exquisite bracelets, girdles, rings, earrings, hairpins, and necklaces, were uncovered from Shilla tombs. They reveal the supreme, artistic craftsmanship that continued to be refined throughout Korean history. The Yi Dynasty also enjoyed a variety of personal ornaments. Some were purely ornamental while others were more for practical purposes.

The women of the Yi Dynasty, unlike Shilla women, adorned themselves with extremely delicate hair ornaments made of gold, silver, and jade with semi-precious

Silver *norigae* with cloisonné (two boys, a needle case, and a cicada as a symbol of rebirth).
Silver.
L. 26cm   W. 32.5cm.
19th c.
The Chang Sook-hwan collection.

Norigae of perfume case (*hyanggap*).
L. 27cm   W. 34cm.
19th c.
The Chang Sook-hwan collection.

stones, pearls, and cloisonné. The hair pins, with fluttering ornaments called *ttuljam*, as a set of three, decorated a ceremonial hairdo, one at the center and on each side. Ornaments in delicate forms of flowers or butterflies were attached to coiled wire from the pin, and fluttered when moved. Delicate and pretty hair pins, called *dwitkkoji* and *muri-kkoji*, decorate *jok* (chignons) of married women. While a *binyuh* (crossbar), played an important role in holding the *jok* in place. This was also made of gold, silver, or jade for summer. The end was embellished with a variety of auspicious designs.

Norigae : Pendant

Norigae, a kind of pendant, came in many different forms and sizes. They were made of a variety of materials, such as gold or silver with one or more semi-precious stones, or with cloisonné. Popular motifs of eggplant, butterflies (symbols of longevity and feminine beauty), geometric designs, or forms of small daggers in decorative cases (*eun-jangdo*), coral, or carved jade with openwork gold, were used. Large pendants with three (*sam-jak*) or five (*o-jak*) ornaments were worn for special ceremonial or festive occasions, while small *norigae* with single pendants were used for informal events. A *norigae* had three parts; a loop of braided, silk string on the top to be suspended from the *goreum* of the *juhgori* or the sash of a skirt, the body which held the decoration in the middle, and one or more long tassel of silk with gold or silver threads. Sometimes, the body was a perfume or a medicine case. All three parts were connected by a most ingenious ways of knotting braided silk cords of red, yellow, or blue with single or multi-colored tassels.

Wearing a jade pendant in the summer, it was believed, took the heat away from the wearer's body. *Norigae* has been valued as one of the most important heirlooms of a family, and handed down from generation to generation.

● *Eun-jangdo* : Silver ornamental dagger

A small, silver dagger hung on a woman's *goreum* or the sash of her skirt as an ornament that guarded a Korean woman's virtue, even to death. Chastity was as important for Korean women as loyalty to the king was for men. Among the strict Confucianism-oriented aristocrats, a woman's chastity was valued much more highly than life itself. It was strictly forbidden to make the dagger longer than 10cm. as it should then be a lethal weapon. Yet it was long enough for a woman to use with deadly results upon herself or sometimes others when her body was tainted and her honor was threatened. Among the aristocrats in old Korea, it carried serious spiritual significance, symbolizing a woman's absolute loyalty to her husband. It is thought that only women carried *eun-jangdo* as an ornament and self-protection, but in fact, gentlemen carried it, too, as a symbol of their loyalty and faithfulness.

Jang-do (amber ornament dagger)
Yi Dynasty
Kim Mihe collection

During the Three Kingdoms period, it was common for a mother to give her daughter an ornamental dagger when she was married, giving her an unspoken message to draw her dagger to fight or even take her life to protect her virtue in the face of a threat, and protect the honor of her husband's family.

Eun-jangdo was most popular during the Koryo Dynasty (918-1392), perhaps due to frequent Mongolian invasions, and gradually became common and eventually a woman's favorite accessory in the Yi Dynasty. Legend says that the wife of magistrate Kim Bum-sok, from Shilla times, plunged a dagger into her bosom and took her life in Hapchuhn in front of the rival General Yungchoon from Paekche in 642 A.D. He had just captured her husband's castle. The general said, "She is indeed a good matron, although from a rival state. She should be laid to rest along with her husband." When Shilla's General Kim Yu-shin retook the castle five years later, he exchanged 800 of his prisoners for the couple's remains, and gave them to their parents in Kyongju, the capital city of Shilla.

The *Tongkuk Shinsok Samkang Haengsildo*, one of a series of commentaries published in 1616 on the manners and morals of Korea, tells how women used their dagger to fight the invading forces of Japanese warlord Toyotomi Hideyoshi from 1592-1597. When the enemy was advancing toward Chungju in central Korea, and as the invaders were nearing her town, magistrate Won Shin's wife carried two daggers, one outside her dress and the other hidden deep inside her jacket. When Chungju was finally captured, and a Japanese officer tried to rape Won Shin's wife, the Japanese officer grabbed her dagger. But she pulled out the other hidden one, stabbed him to death and then took her own life.

A small dagger with a handle and case, which was highly decorated in gold, silver, ivory, white jade, and amber, has been excavated from ancient tombs of Shilla (57 B.C. - A.D. 668) in Kyongju, and areas around Hopchon that were annexed to the Shilla in the 6th century. The ornamental daggers were simply called *jangdo*, and they had many different names depending on the materials used to make the handle and case.

If they were made of *ok* (white-jade),

they were called *ok-jangdo*, and if they were *sanho* (coral), they were called *sanho-jangdo*.

To make the case and handle, artisans would forge or whittle bamboo, the core of a persimmon tree, old jujube wood, aloeswood, Chinese juniper, or copper, silver, gold, white brass, ebony, coral, jade, ivory, amber, agate, malachite, as well as ox-horn and shark skin. A small ring was attached to the case which connected with beautifully braided, colorful, silk cords which tied to the *goreum* or sash of the skirt for women, and waist sash for men. Elaborate motifs of flowers, animals, and landscapes were intricately engraved. But the most cherished were the 10 symbols of longevity. Jade, coral, and hawksbill (turtle shell) *jangdo* were the most expensive and the rarest. These could only be afforded by aristocrats. The most popular material was silver, which was used so often that *eun-jangdo* (silver-*jangdo*) came to represent all *jangdo*. Silver was also used as a food tester, for it would turn black if it came into contact with a poison.

Because of its spiritual significance, the making of an *eun-jangdo* was a delicate and elaborate process that could take as long as three months. It began with tempering quality cast iron for the blade, the life and soul of the dagger. The tempering was the most important step, and demanded the absolute concentration of the swordsmith.

First, the iron was heated with charcoal before being hammered and wrought into shape. During this process, the iron was suddenly cooled a number of times by plunging it into water to harden it or into oil if it was too hard. Proper hardness was important. If it was too hard, then it would snap. If too soft, then it would lose its edge. After hardening, the blade was honed on whetstones and then four Chinese characters that meant "single-minded devotion" were often inscribed on it.

The royal court had their own workshops to produce quality *jangdo* to be used as gifts for courtiers. Private artisans produced *jangdo*, according to the tastes of their aristocrat clients, with different materials and different designs. The skill to make *eun-jangdo*, which requires 10 years to learn, is so near extinction that the Korean government designated it 'Important Intangible Cultural Asset No. 60' in 1978 to preserve the beautiful cultural heritage, although many people nowadays may doubt the justification of the old ethical principles it represents.

Eun-jangdo makers were particular about who they sold to. The story was told that during the Japanese occupation (1910-1945),

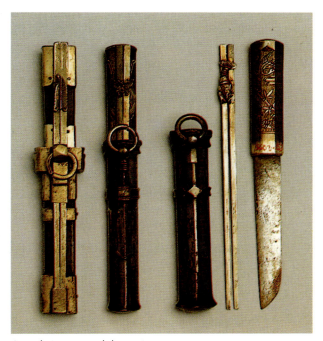

Jang-do (ornamental daggers)
Wood case & handle
L. 14.2 cm Dia. 1.1 cm
Silver case & handle
L. 14 cm   W. 1.8 cm
L. 14.7 cm W. 2 cm
19th c.~ 20th c.
Yi Dynasty.
Ewha Womans Univ. Museum

the governor of South Cholla Province once ordered an *eun-jangdo* from Chang Ik-sung, whose workshop was in Kwangyang, a port city on the south coast in South Cholla Province. Chang, who was in his late 70s, flatly rejected the request by saying, "You lack the qualifications to buy an *eun-jangdo* at any price. Though I'm a grass-roots swordsmith, I won't deal with anybody who has been reduced to a tool of the Japanese in our homeland."

Although the wedding-eve ritual of presenting daggers has disappeared, and the spirit of the dagger is under attack by Confucian tradition, renewed interest in the *eun-jangdo* is rising. The age old craft, fortunately, still exists.

Today, the other best known dagger makers are Yim Won-joong and Park Yong-ki. Yim Won-joong (68) in Suh-dong, Ulsan, South Kyongsang Province, designated as Intangible Cultural Asset in 1993 by the government for his artistry, has been creating *eun-jangdo* since 1946. He was been working 14 hours per day over fifty years.

Park Yong-ki, 64, of South Cholla Province, a master craftsman, and Chang Ik-sung's apprentice, was appointed as a Intangible Cultural Asset by the government in 1978, inheritor of the skill and artistry of *eun-jangdo* making. He was born to a wealthy family, and although sword-smithing was regarded as a low profession, Park Yong-ki began to apprentice under Chang at the age of 14. Park has spent his whole life perfecting his skill, making the exquisitely decorated ornamental daggers. His 50 years of work has been a valuable means of passing on the traditional values of 'loyalty and fidelity' to today's young Koreans. He said, "Loyalty and fidelity are still, and will be forever among the most cherished spiritual values in Korea, as they

were in the days when wearing an *eun-jangdo* was fashionable custom for men and women".

Sool : Tassels and *Maedeup* : Knotting

Decorative tassels were designed for a specific purpose, to be worn by a person of a specific rank, like all Korean clothing and ornaments. The most sumptuous ornaments with tassels were for the royal family, followed by the members of noble families. Tassels were attached at the end of decorative ornaments, *norigae*, which were connected by *maedeup* (knotting) and braided silk cords as draw strings. Tasseled ornaments have a long tradition in Korea.

Koguryo wall paintings, and Koryo as well as Yi Dynasty Buddhist images, all show that tasseled ornaments were worn on clothing, and hung on doors, windows, and blind fittings. The Korean art of braiding and knotting is similar to the Chinese style, but with a distinctively Korean style. The extremely complex way of tying and knotting began with teasing out silk strands to form the thread. Controlling every stage of production, from the dying of the thread or braid, to the weaving of the knot into specific patterns, to the composition of the whole piece, was important. It is still practiced today, mostly by women artists, such as Kim Eun-young. A complete *norigae* enhances the harmony and proportions of the *hanbok*.

Joomuhni : Pouch

Joomuhni, small silk pouches, were worn by everyone to carry necessities, since traditional Korean clothing had no pockets, until the *jokki* (vest) with pockets became popular for men after 1894. A single

Obang-nangja pouch for good fortune with 10 longevity symbols, and fastened by a silk draw string of knots and tassels of five colors.
19.5 x 11.5 cm
The Kim Hee-jin collection

Obang-nang-ja.
19.5 x 11.5 cm
19th c.
The Kim Hee-jin collection.

*Gwi-joomuhni*s
Ewha Womans Univ. Museum, Seoul.

Gwi-joomuhni (angular pouches) embroidered with 5 auspicious characters, 5 stuffed and embroidered triangles, a butterfly, a pomegranate (symbol of many offsprings), a bird, and a drum, had small knife in case (*jang-do*) for self defense, and were suspended from the draw strings.
15.7 x 15.3cm.

*Gwi-joomuhni*s
Ewha Womans Univ. Museum.

122

joomuhni was suspended from the waist-sash of a man by draw strings, and from the sash of a woman's skirt. It was not only an ornament, but had a practical purpose. There were pouches for medicine, perfumes, money, tobacco, calligraphy brushes, and more. The pouches in various shapes were decorated with embroideries, ornamental trinkets, and with silk braided draw strings of knots and tassels. The pouch used by elderly women was called 'a pouch with two ears', because when closed by the draw strings, the folds created ears, the two triangular edges on both sides. Today, *joomuhni* have lost much of their practical function and are regarded more as a decorative accessory.

Joomuhni were made of beautiful, red silk satin, and lined in dark blue or green. Both sides were sewn together (like a pillow-case), and the shape of the bottom two corners made the *joomuhni* either round or square. The way it was folded gave the *joomuhni* a unique shape. It could be a plain pouch with only a plain draw string and tassels, or an elaborately embroidered pouch with motifs like the ten symbols of longevity, and the Chinese characters for happiness, good luck, and long life, tied with braided silk draw strings with tassels and small colorful trinkets. The draw string and tassels were connected by intricate, pretty, artistic, and interesting ways of knotting. The *joomuhni* was, and is, also a popular gift item. There are variety of sizes, colors, and decorations, for men, women, and children.

A *joomuhni* called an *obang-nang-ja* shows the use of five directional colors (blue-east, white-west, red-south, black-north, yellow-central). This system of five colors is based on the *yin-yang-o-haeng* (light and dark, five directional colors) theory of ancient Chinese cosmology for harmonious life.

Beautiful *gwi-joomuhni*s

Cosmetics of the Yi Dynasty

Men's eternal desire for and pursuit of beauty made the use of cosmetics necessary. The cosmetic accessories used during the Yi Dynasty included combs of different size teeth, *bichwi-gae*, used for hair parting, powder cases, *yonjichuhb* (rouge, lipstick containers), peony or camellia hair oil, face mirrors and *kyong-dae* (standing mirrors).

A young woman of marriageable age began with washing her face with red bean soap. Red beans were soaked in water, crushed on millstone, and filtered through hemp cloth. Using this as soap, the face became whiter and softer. To remove thin hairs from the face, two thin, strong strands of thread were used. The threads were soaked in water, covered with sifted, fine,

A fine-toothed bamboo comb

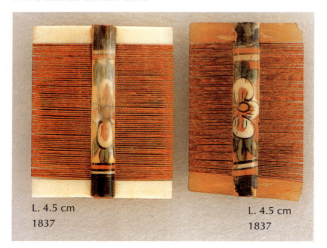

L. 4.5 cm
1837

L. 4.5 cm
1837

Brush to clean combs

L. 6 cm
1780s

L. 6 cm
1837

Spoon for base powder
L. 9 cm
1850

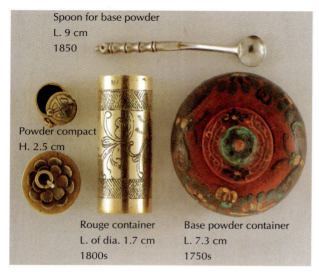

Powder compact
H. 2.5 cm

Rouge container
L. of dia. 1.7 cm
1800s

Base powder container
L. 7.3 cm
1750s

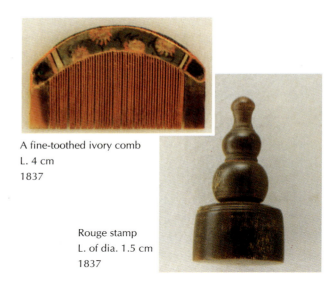

A fine-toothed ivory comb
L. 4 cm
1837

Rouge stamp
L. of dia. 1.5 cm
1837

Brush to clean combs

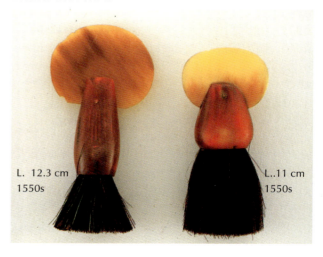

L. 12.3 cm
1550s

L..11 cm
1550s

Different pairs of pincers

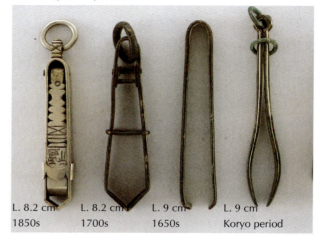

L. 8.2 cm
1850s

L. 8.2 cm
1700s

L. 9 cm
1650s

L. 9 cm
Koryo period

Kyong-dae (standing mirror)
L. 55 cm.
1850s
Suk Joo-sun Folk Art Museum

A painting on the wall of a tomb of the Koguryo period (37 B.C. - 668 A.D.) in North Korea shows red blush on the cheeks of the woman.

A genre painting depicting a woman of the Choson era doing her makeup.

A wall painting from the Anak No. 3 tomb of the Koguryo period showing neatly dressed women with makeup on their cheeks.

pine ashes, and then shaved the face by twisting the threads. Ashes covering the whole face worked as a disinfectant. Then the face was covered with a mixture of honey and pressed garlic, which was cleansed away after waiting a while.

Then face powder, *park-ga boon*, invented by the Park family, was applied. Eye brows were drawn with charcoal in a shape like willow leaves. Finger nails were dyed with a mixture of crushed balsam flower, its new leaves, and alum. This process involved first covering the nail with the mixture, wrapping it with pumpkin leaves, wrapping again with scraps of cloth, and tying the cloth with thread. The cloth was left overnight. After taking it off the next morning, the fingernails were red.

Dress of the Commoners

Dress for Men & Women

The typical everyday clothes for commoners consisted of *chima*, short *juhgori*, *buhsuhn* for women, and *baji*, waist length *juhgori*, *durumagi* (outer coat), *gaht* (horse hair-hat),

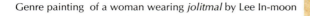

Genre painting of a woman wearing *jolitmal* by Lee In-moon

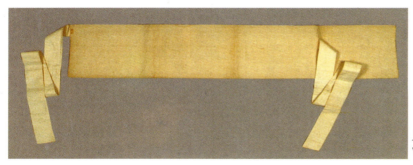

Jolitmal (quilted cotton bust cover). / L. 103 cm W. 26 cm / Yi Dynasty

and *buhsuhn* for men. Dresses were made of cotton, as the cultivation of this plant was officially encouraged, less expensive silk for winter, and hemp or ramie for summer. The winter clothes were lined, and padded with a thin layer of cotton batting for *juhgori*, *baji*, and *durumagi* for further warmth. Sometimes the *juhgori* were quilted. Because the colors of yellow, red, blue, green, and black were reserved for the ruling elite, colors were restricted to neutral, earthy colors.

Although the *durumagi* were basically the same style, they were simpler in overall design and had narrower sleeves than the ceremonial robes worn by aristocrats. *Durumagi* began to be worn by people of all classes, all ages, and women as well, in 1884, when King Gojong (1863-1907) decreed the costume regulation which prohibited expensive, extravagant costumes. It is still worn in various colors and materials as a part of proper attire for men and women. But, of course, padding is no longer needed because of advanced heating systems in the winter time.

Juhgori

During the Yi Dynasty, there were two styles of *juhgori* for women, a small one with a short length and tight sleeves, and another one with a long length and large sleeves. In later periods, the chest band, called *jolitmal*, appeared to cover the armpit and to tighten the chest compensating for a ridiculously small *juhgori*. It was made of cotton or *myungju* (soft silk) of .33m width, worn under the *juhgori*, and padded in the winter. Men's *juhgori* style stayed on.

Often used by commoners were *toshi* (wristlets), which were lined and padded for the winter, and woven with bamboo strips or wisteria vines in the summer for better ventilation and protection from sweat.

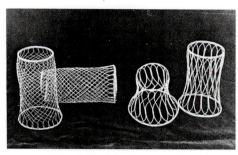

Toshi. Bamboo

Baji : Trouser

The *baji*, the voluminous men's trouser, folded (one-fold to the leftward) in front, belted at the waist with a sash, and tied at the ankles over the buhsuhn (Korean cotton socks).

They were extremely comfortable when sitting on silk cushions on ondol in the lotus position.

Baji & juhgori
1930s / Suk Joo-sun Folk Art Museum, Seoul

According to the Korean concept of the human body, the waist expands after a person has eaten, contracts if one is hungry or not in good health, and is always in flux. Therefore, *baji* were designed in one large size to be worn by anyone just by folding in or folding out as one's waistline required. Clothes were to be flexible, worn for comfort, representing the flexible attitude of Koreans have towards material things.

The style of men's *baji* did not change over the years (except for narrow work trousers). There are voluminous trousers and very narrow tight ones on the mural paintings of Koguryo Tombs. These baggy trousers were unlined in the summer, lined in the spring and fall, and lined and padded with a thin layer of cotton batting in the winter. Again, no padding is needed today with advanced heating systems.

Jokki : Vest with pockets

The *jokki* came much later in the Yi Dynasty. The *jokki* had three pockets, a smaller one above a larger one. Its buttons were flat with flowers, butterflies, or geometric designs. It was lined with different materials and color, and worn by men over the *juhgori* and under the *magoja*. Women wore *baeja*, a vest without pockets or fastenings, which was lined and bordered with fur.

Magoja : Outer-jacket

Magoja resembled *juhgori*, but closed at the center by weighty buttons of silver, gold, jade, or amber in the shape of a tear drop that went through a loop made of the same material as the *magoja* or of braided silk thread. It had no collars, and had a short slit on both sides. It was lined and worn by both men and women of all ages.

The *magoja* was originally worn as an outer jacket by Manchurians. In 1887, when the ex-Regent Daewon-goon was freed from a Chinese prison (1882-1887), he returned home wearing a *magoja* and it began to spread. It was an outer jacket used in cold weather areas for better warmth. It eventually was worn by women as well.

Woman's and girl's brocade *baeja* lined with fur to be worn over *juhgori*.
S. Yang's Collection

Rich *yang-dan magoja* & *chima* by Park Sun-young

Women's silk *sa magoja*
33 x 123 cm
20th c.
Suk Joo sun Folk Art Museum
※ It was worn on a woman's 60th birthday only if her parents are still alive.

Durumagi : Outer-coat

The *durumagi* was worn by upper class men even before the Three Kingdoms period, and developed into various styles such as *tchang-ui* and *dopo*, all with large flowing sleeves. Later in the Yi Dynasty, the much modified version of this became the *durumagi*, worn by all as part of the proper attire for formal occasions. It had narrower sleeves and *goreum* which tied at the right side of the chest, instead of the chest-band. It was worn for both warmth and appropriateness.

To make *durumagi*, the same amount of material as for *chima-juhgori*, was needed. Two triangular pieces of the same material, *moo* (gussets) were attached on each side from the armpit to the hem, making a flare effect for freedom and better mobility. *Yangban* used either plain or luxuriously patterned silk brocade, satin, or soft silk.

The *durumagi* were lined, and padded with a thin layer of cotton batting in the winter for further warmth. They used fine cotton, which was lined, for spring and fall, and used fine, light weight, unlined ramie, linen, *sa*, or *ra* for the summer. Later, wool gabardine became very popular for warmth and practicality as winter wear. In earlier

Ringe in blue silk brocade *durumagi*

periods, the commoners were restricted by law as well as resources to rough hemp and cotton garments at best. As for colors, the *yangban* could choose a wide variety of bright colors while commoners were not allowed certain colors. But today there is no limit in choosing of color and material.

Underwear for Women

Unlike men's wear, women's wear changed a little by the fashion trends of the time. The women's costumes included *juhgori*, *chima*, *nae-ui* (under-wear), *yaebok* (ceremonial dress), *sseugae* (head-gear) and *jangshingu* (accessories). But, to satisfy women's desire to make the bottom skirt look extremely voluminous, underwear developed.

The *chima* was given a full silhouette by wearing seven or eight layers of underwear. To be able to cover this volume, 12 *pok* (a counter for strips of cloth) *chima*, with narrow pleats, were required while wearing tiny *juhgori* with extremely tight sleeves that almost stopped blood circulation. Women of the Yi Dynasty *yangban* class had a special interest in underwear. Interestingly, the *sok-jucksam*, worn under the *juhgori*, was developed to be worn as an outer summer jacket, commonly called *jucksam*.

Dari-sok-ot (basic underwear) was made of cotton in any season, and *sok-sok-ot* (bloomers) were made of soft cotton or *myungju* in the winter, and hemp or ramie in the summer. *Baji*, worn as outer and inner wear during the Three Kingdoms period, became underwear in various styles for women during the Yi Dynasty. *Dan-sok-ot* was worn right under the skirt. It was made with great care in the choice of material and sewing, for it showed between the wrap-around *chima*. Sashes, cloth knots, braided thread, or loops were used to close undergarments. No zippers were used.

Notably, upper class women wore additional underskirts, *mujigi* (three to seven tiers of underskirts), indicating their increasing desire for further volume.

However, the custom of underwear began to change from the 1920s, simplifying *dari-sok-ot* and *sok-sok-ot* (bloomers or culottes) to panties, and *dan-sok-ot* and *mujigi* became *sok-chima* (slips).

☙ Process of making *hanbok*

The process of making clothes was usually done by women. *Juhgori*, *baji*, *chima*, and all others were cut separately on a flat surface according to the approximate size. A young woman's first lesson at home was to learn how to sew and embroider, while a young boy of about the same age was sent to the *suh-dang* (private school) to learn Chinese classics, and begin the preparation of becoming a Confucian scholar. Thus, Yi Dynasty women considered needles a very important item in their daily life. Needles were kept in ornamental cases which were even worn as pendants (*norigae*), tied to

Sok-ot (women's silk *sa* underwear)
Ewha Womans Univ. Museum, Seoul

juhgori goreum or skirt sashes. Measuring sticks, scissors, needles, thread, thimbles, soldering irons, and press irons were referred to as the "seven friends" of the women's room.

Sewing box (thread spools, silver needle case, bamboo ruler case, thimbles, etc.) / 19th c.

Silk thimbles with embroidery. / 19th c.

Headdress for Common Women

From the earliest times, headdress has been either utilitarian or a symbol of status, representing a fixed role in society. Matrons in tight-fitting *jobawi*, scholarly gentlemen in *gahts*, and royalty in crowns, made a statement with the hats they wore. However the social significance and symbolism of hats has changed in the 20th century.

Muhri-suguhn : Head scarves

Commoner women often wrapped their heads in cold weather with white scarves of plain cotton or *myungju* (sheer silk), and padded with a thin layer of cotton batting.

The method of wrapping differed from one province to another. The tomb mural painting from Gakjuh-chong in Tunggu of the Koguryo Kingdom (37 B.C. - 668 A.D.) shows women wearing these scarves, indicating that the use of scarves has been a long tradition. In the Gakjuh-chong mural, the scarves covered the hair and head completely, while the Ssangyong-chong mural shows the head covered only partially, showing another way of wearing the scarves.

The purpose of wearing *muhri-suguhn* was more practical. It kept the hair from falling down, and protected it from the sun and cold wind better than other hats worn for etiquette and decoration. The Northern province of Pyongan, and Hwanghae used a rectangular scarf folded in four layers

Woman wearing *muhri-suguhn* (head scarf) & *gomooshin*

lengthwise, covering the entire head, and tying at the back. The people in Kaesong (east-central Korea) used square *myungju* (sheer silk) folded in half and tied at the back. The people in Kangwon province (west-central Korea) used square scarves folded into triangles, covering the head then tucked in, instead of tied.

Jang-ot : *Durumagi*-like cloak

Jang-ot, this unusual garment literally means long clothes. It was born out of the tradition of segregating males and females at the age of seven during the Yi Dynasty. They were not supposed to come face to face even when they had to talk. This continued until the time of the growing western influence at the turn of the century.

The *jang-ot* could be easily mistaken as an outer-coat (*durumagi*), but was slightly different in design. This pleated cloak was worn by common women over the head to hide their faces. It barely showed the face in order to protect a lady's modesty when going out. It was gathered and attached by sashes which were held by hand, not tied, under the chin. It puffed round the face when worn, allowing the wearer to peep out. Even upper class women wearing a *jang-ot* were able to escape the seclusion of the home for a walks or visits, usually at night. The favored materials were *myungju* (sheer silk) in the winter, and stiffened *sa* (silk gauze) in the summer, usually in red or jade green, and unlined for very hot weather. Koryo women used a similar headgear called *mongsoo*, which showed the wearer's face and looked more natural. This was used by women of all classes.

"Beautiful woman wearing *jang-ot* ", by Park Yun-ok
Water-color painting / 1997

Jang-ot
L. 111 cm. / W. of sleeves 67 cm / 1830s
Suk Joo-sun Folk Art Museum

A man wearing *jipshin* with *hanbok*

Shin-bal : Shoes

Koreans wore shoes in the first century B.C. (Ma-han period) according to historical records, when *jipshin* (straw sandals) were worn by men and women. There were *jipshin* made of various straw, bulrush, dried inner bark of arrowroot, hemp (or ramie), and even paper (durable rice paper from mulberry trees). Rain shoes were made from wood (*mok-shin*) and *Yoohye* (leather shoes preserved with oil for waterproofing).

Jipshin : Straw sandal

Jipshin were worn by commoners as everyday footwear from the Three-Han period. *Jipshin* were made by weaving coarse straw, or the dried inner bark of arrowroot, or durable, rice paper, strands from mulberry bark which was twisted, layered, glued together, and oiled. But it could not be worn in wet weather. So, today only mourners at funerals use these straw sandals.

Mituri : Hemp or ramie sandal

Mituri was made the same way as *jipshin*, but woven with raw fibers of ramie or hemp. These shoes provided rather smooth and light footwear for commoners, and later noble men also wore them. Only skilled craftsmen could make this kind of high quality shoe which had various color

Jipshin (straw shoes).
19th c.

Mok-shin covered with silk with elevated sole with double.

Woon-pi hye (deer skin covered man's shoes)

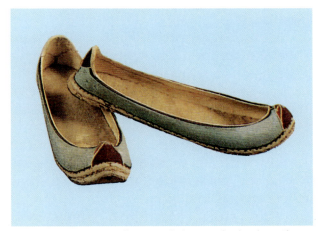

Woon-hye (woman's silk covered shoes with cloud motif on toes & heels)

Heuk-hye (black felt covered man's shoes)

Woon-hye (woman's silk covered shoes with cloud motif on toes & heels)

135

combinations, and could be worn only in dry weather.

Mok-shin : Wooden clogs

Mok-shin (*namu-shin*) were chiseled out of a single piece of light wood in the same shape as up-turned toe shoes. They had elevated soles on a double support, which was ideal for muddy roads, and was used also as rain shoes. The original shape is unknown, but it probably had strings for tying and the double support must have been a later idea. Because of its lack of flexibility it could not be used for long distance walking, and lost popularity.

For the Korean word *shin-bal*, *shin* means shoe and *bal* means foot. Interestingly, the Korean cotton socks, *buhsuhn*, were made to custom-fit each foot by adjusting the fold of the center seams, while the *shin-bal* could be worn on either foot.

Shoes in the shape of Native American canoes with up-turned toes were in use during the Shilla period, as shown on stone relief carvings in a grotto of Shinson Temple on the Tansok Mountain slopes near Kyongju. The government has designated these relief carvings as a national treasure.

The up-turned toe shoes for women were narrower and more pointed than men's which had wide, round, and flat toes. This style of shoes is unique to Korea, and can not be seen historically anywhere else including China or Japan.

In dry weather, when Korean people dressed-up, men wore the more luxurious *taesahye*, and women wore *danghye* in various colors and silk materials. These were worn only by the upper class in earlier times.

Korean Saying about Clothing

"Every beggar has a day to see his guest"

Even a poor person may be called on by a visitor, whom he should receive in a proper dress. So, he must have a proper set of clothing.

"A dressed beggar can get food, but a naked beggar cannot"

Clothing is very important even to a beggar; Clothes make the man.

"Dressed in brocade and strolling in the dark"

Nobody will notice a magnificently dressed person in the dark; a useless effort.

"Coarse linen is better than no linen at all"

This is said of the poor people who have no other choice but linen while the rich can afford silk all the time.

"Clothing are your wings"

Dress for success.

Dress for other members

Heuk-ui : Servants' wear

Male servants at the royal court, and in noble households, wore a *baji-juhgori* of rough, white cotton. The *baji* was tied at the waist under the *juhgori*, at the ankle, and below the knee with a sash for better mobility. A *heuk-ui* (black narrow coat) with a white neck band was joined at the end of the neck band in the front center, without overlapping, by a very short, narrow sash. Both sides opened from the armpit all the way down to the hem, so that the two front panels could be pulled back to tie loosely for easier movement.

Female servants wore a big, white apron, like a smaller version of the *chima*, but long enough in length to cover the front of *chima*. Usually, shoes worn by male and female servants were made of straw. A rather small, black *gaht*, with a very narrow brim, was worn by male servants.

Genre painting by Hye-won (Shin Yun-bok)
A Lady with male & female servants

Juhgori 1910s / *Chima* 1920s / Front apron 1930s

Heuk-ui. (cotton) for male servants
19th c.
National Folk Arts Museum, Seoul

Farmer's Wear

Farmers were clad in plain, white cotton, rough hemp or linen. They wore *sat-gaht*, a big, cone-shaped hat, made of either bamboo or reed, to protect against the hot sun or rain when they were in the fields working, and *jipshin* (straw shoes). Like a servant's outfit, the *baji* was tied right below the knee for better mobility. This basic outfit did not change, as the *yangban* and courtier's costumes did over the years.

The ingenious farmer's rain coat (*dorong-ee*) of the Yi Dynasty was made of straw or grass which was attached to a base of string netting. It was worn over the shoulder like a cape, and tied under the chin in front. Another *dorong-ee* was worn at the waist, like a skirt, to protect the lower body from the rain. Both were worn over the basic *baji-juhgori*.

Rendez-vous on the Road by Hye-won, Shin Yun-bok

Sat-gaht (farmer's hat).
Bamboo or reed.
H.35 cm.
19th c.
Suk Joo-sun Museum, Seoul

Dorong-ee (straw farmer's rain coat).
19th c. Suk Joo-sun Museum, Seoul

Mareun-shin

Gapju : Armor

Dusuk-rin-gapju was armor fortified with square brass scales connected in regular rows for flexibility. It covered the shoulders, upper arms, front and back to the hips, and was worn by the commander-in-chief.

This round, neck lined armor was bordered with fur. The lower part was fortified with brass or iron studs, closed at the front center, and fastened with a wide, indigo blue sash at the chest. The wristlet of leather was also reinforced with brass or iron studs. This armor, with a slit opening from the waist down on both sides, was worn over a rich, cloud-figured, black brocade inner coat. The helmet, of four iron plates in black and decorated with gold phoenix designs, was topped by a tasseled trident. The ear flaps and the back flap were reinforced with brass scales and bordered with fur. Black, deer skin boots trimmed in red and white were worn, and a baton of wisteria wood was carried.

Pi-gap : Leather lined armor of the officers

This knee length armor had short sleeves, a round neck line, and an opening from the waist down at the sides, and in front and back for better mobility. It was held together by an indigo blue sash (*juhndae*), and worn over a black skirt, gray trousers, and a red jacket.

The armor was decorated with yellowish orange cotton, stenciled with flowers and scrolling vines (*bosanghwa-dangcho-muni*), lined with white cotton, fortified inside with

Dusuk-rin-gapju (Brass & iron armor).
L. 103cm. W. 122cm.
19th c. Korea Univ. Museum, Seoul.

Pi-gap (Brass scales armor).
19th c. Kyongju National Museum, Kyongju

scraps of ox or hog skin, and sequined outside with iron or brass. It also had ear flaps, a back flap, and wristlets.

A simpler, four plate, iron helmet with a trident, and black, deerskin boots with yellow trimming were worn. A sword was held in hand.

Dress of the Monks

The *heukjangsam* and *gasa* were full dress for Buddhist monks for various ceremonies, services, devotions and Zen meditations. The *heukjangsam* (robe) was made of cotton or hemp in black. It had a square collar, large sleeves, and resembled a *durumagi* without a *dongjuhng* (white neck band). It had an additional pleat, symbolizing penance, between the front opening, and a gusset from both sides of the armpit, which made it different from the *durumagi* of laymen. It was worn over the basic *baji-juhgori*.

The *gasa* (outer shawl) was worn over *heukjangsam*. *Gasa* was the most typical and significant part of a Buddhist monk's clothes. This outer garment was originally designed to receive food when begging for alms by a monk, but it became a grade badge, the higher the rank, the greater number of columns in the design of the *gasa*, the highest being 25 columns (25-*jo*). It was rectilinear in its shape, broad, lined, and flat. The *gasa* was worn over the left shoulder, and tied under the right arm at the waist, like a shawl. The *gasa* has basically

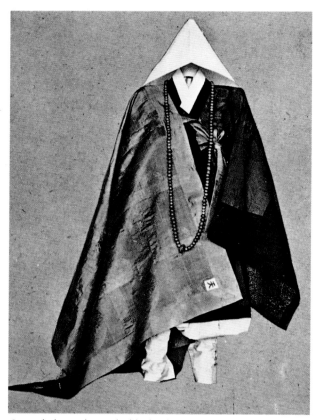

Seung-bok (monk's outfit), black robe, *gasa*, and *gokkal* (hat).
Suk Joo-sun Museum, Seoul

Nab-ui (Monk's regular robe, usually worn when monk goes out to ask for an alms)
19th c.

Gasa (*Junkeumran gasa*) bestowed to the monk, *Jajang-bupsa* by Shilla's 27th ruler, Queen Sunduhk in 645 (year 19 of Taejong of Tang China).
L. 85cm.
W. 152cm. (24 *jo*).
Shilla.
Yuam-sa (temple)
Suk Joo-sun Museum, Seoul

remained unchanged since the beginning of Buddhism from the 6th century B.C., in India, where the prince who became Buddha (the "Enlightened One") lived. According to Buddhist texts, the most appropriate material for the making of the *gasa* were soiled and discarded small scraps of cloth collected from waste heaps and stitched together. The *gasa* was made by sewing these cloths in many horizontal and vertical stripes in a columnar format. Buddhist texts indicate that Buddha instructed a disciple, *Ahnan*, to design a garment, based on the ordered rows of a rice field, for the monks. This symbolized the furrows of mental cultivation, while the number of rows indicated the Buddhist rank of its wearer.

Later, variations developed to distinguish the clergy of different sects, such as *son* (Zen or Chokae sect), which used a simpler more humble *gasa*, while others used more colorful ones. The *gasa* also symbolized Buddhist learning and its physical transmission from teacher to disciple, which became an important event in the propagation of the faith. The colors were always neutral, irregular, and odd, such as a shabby black, bluish green, or brown.

A typical costume of the Buddhist monk consisted of *jangsam, gasa, yunhwagwan* (lotus-shape cap), or *gokkal* (folded, pointed hat), a *yum-jool* (prayer necklace) around the neck, a *mok-tak* (small wooden gong) in hand, *baekmal* (white Korean cotton socks), *haengjon* (leggings), and *jipshin*. The *yum-jool* was made of 108 beads, as 108 scraps of cloth were patched to make a *gasa*. This stood for the 108 agonies of the world. A monk meditated to forget these agonies, and thus attain Buddhahood (enter Nirvana). The *gasa* was embroidered with Chinese characters representing *tchun* (heaven), *wang* (king), *hae* (sun), and *dal* (moon) enclosed in medallions. The *heukjangchae* with a red *gasa* was a sacerdotal robe. The monk's clothing has changed little over thousands of years, from the time of the mid-Three Kingdoms period to the end of the Koryo. The current monk's costume

Song-lark and *go-kkal* (hats). / Genre painting by Hye-won. / 19th c.

in Korea is a gray outer coat with a brown *gasa*. Currently, there is no 'code of law', but the *chokae* sect (Son or Zen) is planning to establish the 'code of law' for monk's costume.

◐ *Seungmoo* : **Buddhist monk's dance**

Buddhist ceremonial dances probably came from China along with Buddhist teachings. As Buddhism replaced folk religion firmly during the Koryo period considerable court music and dance were imported from China for Buddhist rituals. The dances were for supplication to Buddha so that deceased souls may easily enter Nirvana (paradise), or were ceremonies such as *Jumansik* which drive away evil spirits and are performed by a married sect of priests.

However, it was generally believed that the nun's dance had more shamanistic influences than Buddhist, both emotionally and technically, in spite of its title and the costume of the dancer. As the dance continued to evolve through its long history, shamanistic elements were combined with Buddhist-style props.

Because of the Confucian oriented Yi Dynasty's persecution of Buddhism, monks used musical chanting of scriptures and dance performances in order to appeal to a wider public. These became an important part of rituals in the temple.

Nuns wore a white, conical, silk gauze cap covering half of the face, white *juhgori*, blue *chima*, a white silk gauze outer robe which was shorter than the skirt and had long white sleeves, white cotton socks. A long, wide, red silk gauze sash (modified version of *gasa*) worn over the left shoulder was tied at the right side of the waist. The slow, dramatic and solemn movements of their dance are delicate, mysterious and yet very powerful. Thus symbolize heaven, earth, and human beings in harmony according to the laws of nature.

Seungmoo dancer, Lee Ae-ju, designated as Intangible Cultural Asset No. 57.
A leading *seungmoo* performer and professor of Korean traditional dance at Seoul National Univ.

Lee Mae-bang, a leading *seungmoo* performer and professor of Korean traditional dance at Ewha Womans Univ. in his silk costume, he designed and sewn. He was designated for his performance as Intangible Cultural Asset No. 27.

Seungmoo dancer Lee Mae-bang dancing in full costume which he designed.

145

⬤ *Gisaeng* : Professional entertainer

Traditionally, most of the Korean court dances were performed only by men, but if the dancers were female, they were the royal *gisaeng*. An important feature of Korean dance during the Koryo period was the *gisaeng* institute. It was established before the Unified Shilla period when the king established an institution called *Wonhwa* (original flowers). *Gisaeng* were a professional group of women court entertainers. They were women of good moral character, who sang and danced for the Shilla. They may have been the first recorded court entertainers.

The *gisaeng* were beautiful and charming women who were trained from an early age how to sing, dance, and play musical instruments, according to their talent. Young girls of 10~15 years of age who were chosen to become *gisaeng* started with music lessons. They were well-read and versed in literature, and wrote poems. In addition, they were good artists. The most well known *gisaeng*, for her beauty and her poetry, is Hwang Jin-ee.

During the reign of King Sungjong of the Yi Dynasty, a young girl called Kyoung-ee, who was a servant of humble origins, became a *gisaeng*. She was able to raise her social status by becoming a concubine because of her musical talent as a singer.

Because of their contact as entertainers with artists, scholars and rulers of the nation, they became the most highly

Hair Arranging Women Entertainers.
Genre painting by Shi San (Yoo Un-hong)
18th c.

A *gisaeng* house, with customers
Genre painting by Hye-won, 18th c.

Rendezvous by full moonlight
Genre painting by Hye-won, 18th c.

Boating Scene on the Han River, three scholars and three *gisaeng*
Genre painting by Hye-won, 18th c.

Three *gisaeng* and three males beside a lotus pond enjoying *gayageum* music.
Genre painting by Hye-won, 18th c.

Gisaeng performing Sword Dance before customers
Genre painting by Hye-won (Shin Yoon-bok)

cultured and educated women of the country. In a highly restricted society, especially for women, they had a remarkable amount of social freedom. They were not prostitutes and often they performed a wife's role, hosting the guests of their regular customers. According to historical records, the court mobilized *gisaeng* to entertain envoys, appointing the most qualified *gisaeng* for the most important envoys. Thus, *gisaeng* also played important roles in the diplomatic community.

Furthermore, *gisaeng* played an important part in carrying on valuable Korean traditions in literature, painting, and music. From the initial period of the Koryo dynasty, remained under the patronage and protection of the crown.

The *gisaeng* dressed in a bright green robe decorated with rich floral designs over a luxurious, crimson, silk skirt. A wide band around her chest tied at the back. Usually, when they danced the *gisaeng* would wear bright, red silk, full, loose-fitting, wrap-around skirts with equally vibrant, yellow, silk jackets with dark red collars, sleeve cuffs, and tie-ribbons. Both hands were covered by extra long, white, tube-like *hansam*, an extension of the multi-colored sleeve of the green robe. On their head was a small, gaily decorated crown with fluttering ornaments of semi-precious stones which shimmered by the slightest movement. Their smooth, glossy, black hair was drawn tightly into a bun at the nape of the neck, and secured by a large gold crossbar with precious stones terminating at one end in the shape of flowers or birds. Two very large, red silk ribbons, with gold-leaf imprints of floral designs, were hung from the crossbar onto the *gisaeng*'s back. When *gisaeng* performed, it was truly dazzling and impressive.

Street wear of the *gisaeng* consisted of a light green, soft silk jacket with ribbons, sleeve cuffs, a collar in a contrasting dark red, and an unlined skirt of pale pink, soft silk. The skirt wrapped on the right side, indicating their social standing. They wore wide, felt hats in the shape of small umbrellas, which were constructed with 14 to 16 spokes, covered with perilla oiled mulberry paper (rice paper), and decorated with flower designs, butterflies and Chinese characters for good luck and longevity. The hat was tied under the chin by wide ribbons. They completed their attire by wearing red leather shoes.

Royal patronage of court entertainment ended with Japan's annexation of Korea in 1910. However, the *gisaeng* culture passed from Korea to Japan where it became known as *geisha* (meaning accomplished person).

Thus, after the fall of the Yi Dynasty in Korea, *gisaeng* were driven from the palace, and their reputation collapsed. The best they could hope for was to become the concubine of wealthy businessmen or government official, or open up a small business (tea house or restaurant) of their own with the financial support of former clients. Kim Young-han, the last surviving *gisaeng* of the Yi Dynasty, became a *gisaeng* because her *yangban* family experienced financial difficulties. During her life as a *gisaeng*, she befriended the famous poet, Paik Suk. She recently contributed an enormous amount of money to Buddhist temples.

◖ Shamanism

Shamanism, an old folk religion, had links with northeastern Asian regions, Manchuria, and Siberia, and strongly influenced the development of Korean culture. Neolithic Age people believed in animism, and thought all natural objects had spirits. The *Chuhnshin* (sky-god), and *Sushin* (water-god) symbolized by the dragon, *Sanshin* (mountain-god), *Toshin* (earth-god), and *Kwishin* (wandering ghost) symbolizing the souls of the unfortunate, had to be propitiated by sacrifices.

Primitive Koreans were curious by the things around them and wondered if, like humans, other things also had spirits. They attempted to understand, and if possible, to come to terms with their environment. Their search eventually evolved into a belief that spirits reside in the animate and inanimate objects around them. They believed that a good peaceful life lay in proper relations between spirits and humans, and required an intermediary who could speak to the spirit, expel bad luck, cure sickness, and assure a propitious passage from this world to the next when the time came. Thus a *mudang* (shaman), an intermediary, would be called upon to perform rituals. Originally, Shamanism in Korea was probably the religion of clans, and the clan leader might have been the shaman.

Nowadays, the Shaman is invariably a woman, unlike in the past when the shaman could be either male or female. The shaman profession can be passed on by heredity or brought on by a kind of calling. When she starts, the Shaman acquires cult objects such as a curved dagger, mirror, and drum. When she communicates with the spirit, she falls into a trance by chanting, acting and dancing. She performs *goot* (rituals), accompanied by a drum with an exuberant rhythm and ear-splitting noise, which is enough to drive away all the evil spirits and invoke good. She tries to rout out problems and find solutions for them. Such rituals usually take place under spirit-trees or spirit-rocks. The clients supply the offerings such as chicken, grains, or cloth. Unlike other religions' dance ceremonies, *goot* (shaman rituals) incorporate humor and satire. Even today, in spite of high technology, in modern metropolitan cities like Seoul, some Koreans are still seeking their favorite *mudang*.

During the Yi Dynasty, shamans were dressed in *Munyo-bok* (a long, black, unlined, silk, sleeveless outer robe for rites). It was worn over an inner coat of yellow silk with red sleeves, and a red silk skirt underneath.

The outer wear was open in the front, the back from a high waist, and on both sides from the armpit. It was fastened at the back with an indigo blue sash that wrapped around the chest. She wore a hat with pheasant plumes and hanging loops of amber, coral, and quartz beads; it was, tied under the chin with a sash in a bow. When performing rites for a tutelary god, they wore a low-top hat and red leather shoes. The tutelary gods were believed to be

'Dancing Shaman' performing the *Goot*
Genre painting by Hye-won.
Late Yi Dynasty
※ Among the audience, one woman is wearing *jang-ot*.

dwelling among people and needed to be appeased constantly so that people could lead a peaceful and prosperous life in harmony.

Fans, rattles, and clinking, ornate, curved daggers whirling in their hands symbolized a shaman's power in expelling evil spirits. The rite was characterized by dynamic dances, and accompanied by drums, gongs, and cymbals. The rite consisted of the shaman praying for good fortunes or foretelling good and/or bad luck as an intermediary between the spirits, the supernatural, and humans.

During the Yi Dynasty, shamanist rites were practiced often at the royal palace.

Costume for Special Occasions

Clothes for Children

Traditionally, a newborn baby was kept in a baby wrapper of soft cotton for the first seven days, then changed into a white, soft cotton or silk *baenae-juhgori* (jacket), long enough to cover the baby, which was tied in the front with a string of seven strands of cotton thread, regardless of sex. Two months after the birth, a baby-skirt, *dorong-ee*, with an opening at the bottom for diaper changes, was worn with a *juhgori*.

For the first birthday, boys wore a bright costume of silk *saektong juhgori* (multi-colored striped sleeves), a *baji* in pretty colored purple, a dark blue *jokki* (vest), a *gachi durumagi* (outer coat with *saektong* sleeves), and a *juhnbok* (unlined, sleeveless, black stiffened silk gauze, long vest) tied with a silk braided cord at the chest. Also, a boy wore a *bokkuhn* (a turban-like, black hood) on his first birthday. It was made of stiffened, *sa* (silk gauze), tied in back with an embroidered sash, and was decorated with gold or silver leaf imprints of auspicious motifs for longevity and happiness. With it he wore embroidered, white cotton socks with up-turned toes, which were lined, padded, and quilted for the winter, with red silk tassels at the toes, and ribbons tied around the ankle to keep the socks in place. A pair of flower patterned shoes completed his attire.

Girls wore silk *saektong juhgori*, red silk chima, colorfully embroidered *buhsuhn*, and *jobawi* (tight-fitting, lined, black silk hats with a top opening) or a *jogdoori* (small, black silk crown with ornaments). A pair of tasseled Korean socks and flower-embroidered silk shoes completed the attire for outings.

The *gachi durumagi* (children's outer robe) was a colorful, *dan* (silk damask) robe which was lined with red or white for winter, or made unlined with stiffened silk gauze for warmer weather. It had long, five-colored *saektong* sleeves, and an indigo blue collar and *goreum* for boys, and a dark red collar for girls. It was worn by children on their first birthday and New Years celebration outings as part of a formal ensemble until the age of six. It was worn over *baji-juhgori*, under a sleeveless, long, silk gauze outer robe and tied with a wide, embroidered sash for boys. Girls wore it over *chima-juhgori*.

The *saektong* (five colors) represented *obang-wi* (5 primary substances or elements of cosmology) and *obang-haeng* (5 directions, east, west, north, south and center). This symbolized good harmony, and was believed to protect children from illness and bad luck, and ensure them a healthy long life.

Modified version of girl's birthday att
by Lee Young-hee

A boy and girl in first birthday attire, 20th c.

Gachi durumagi for girl (ceremonial robe for the 1st birthday)
Green silk damask *gil* (bodice), multi colored patch worked front lapels, red *git* (collar), *goreum* (ribbons) and sleeve cuffs with embroidery.
L. 60 cm. / W. of sleeves. 41.5 cm.
1920 / Ewha Womans Univ. Museum, Seoul

Gachi durumagi for boy
Green silk damask *gil* (bodice), yellow *sup* (front lapels), red *mu* (gusset), indigo blue *git* (collar) and *goreum* (tie ribbons) and crisp white *dongjuhng* (neckband).
L. 59.5cm. / W. 35.5cm.
20th c. / Suk Joo-sun Museum, Seoul

Girls and boys in *han*
by Lee Young-hee

Obangjang durumagi
Ewha Womans University Museum, Seoul

Juhnbok
Sleeveless green *sa* robe for boys for their 1st birthday
L. 58 cm
Ewha Womans Univ. Museum, Seoul

Wedding Attire

Wedding attire for the bride and groom was made of very elaborate and colorful material, as the wedding was considered one of the most important events in one's life in Korea.

The groom wore *samo-gwan-dae*. *Samo* was a black, stiffened silk, gauze hat with side-flaps, which was originally worn by officials. Grooms were allowed to wear these on the special occasion of their wedding ceremony once in their life time. *Gwan-dae*, the formal robe and girdle of the courtiers of civil and military offices was worn over basic *juhgori* and *baji* for wedding ceremonies. This attire is still widely worn.

The robe, *tanryong*, with a rounded neck line and wide sleeves, was made of silk brocade and woven with cloud figures and flowers in various colors. A *dae* was worn over the robe. The emblematic square with a pair of cranes and auspicious embroidered symbols was used by the courtiers of the civil service and was attached in the front and back. A square, thin, stiffened silk gauze fan was held open in both hands, and was raised up to veil his face when the bridegroom entered the ceremonial hall. Black, deer skin, and ankle-length boots with red trimmings were worn. The *samo* (hat) was stuffed with supportive wire strings or bamboo strips, mounted with horse-hair, and bent into shape.

Traditional wedding picture
1930s
Cynthia Tennent Sohn Collection

Reenactment of Queen Min's (*Myungsung-hwanghoo*) Wedding Ceremony held at Woonhyun Palace in 1997

onsam front view (L), *hwal-ot* & man in *hong-yongpo*
worn for the Fashion Show at the Washington, D.C.
Huh Young

157

Reenactment of Myungsung Hwang-hoo's wedding held at Woonhyun Palace in 1997

The bride wore a *nok-wonsam* (green bridal robe), which was originally worn by princesses, daughters of noblemen, and queen consorts for minor ceremonies. But the commoner bride's *nok-wonsam* was devoid of ornate gold-leaf imprints and embroideries. However, a chest band with either simple gold-leaf imprints or embroideries was allowed to be worn by the commoner. It was worn over the red silk *chima* and yellow *juhgori*. As a commoner she was allowed to wear it for her wedding only once in her life time. During the Yi Dynasty, this style robe was worn for weddings by various social classes, but the status of the wearer was always clearly declared by color and decorative patterns. The wedding robes of high born women were heavily decorated with various auspicious motifs symbolizing a happy marriage. On her head, a simpler *binyuh* (crossbar) to hold a chignon with front and back ribbons, and a *jogdoori* was worn. A *hansam* (extra long, soft, white, doubled silk cloth) was draped over the bride's hands.

For weddings, the bride had her first special hairdo, *jok* (chignon), as a married woman. The hair was parted at the center first, braided, tied with red silk *daenggi* (ribbons), gathered into a bun at the nape of the neck, fastened with a very long *binyuh* (crossbar of gold or jade, terminated in a beautifully decorated, dragon head, phoenix, or other design), and decorated with two *ttuljam* (ornate fluttering hair pins), and two black *doturak-daenggi* (large silk ribbons with gold-leaf imprints) suspended to drape in front at the neck, and two floor-length *dae-daenggi* (large ribbons which hung from the chignon and draped over the *binyuh*, in back). A *jogdoori* (a small, pill-box shaped, black, silk covered, jeweled crown) was worn on top of the head, and tied by two ribbons under the chignon behind the ears. Two or three *norigae* (gold or jade pendants with silk knots and strings with tassels) were suspended from the sash of the skirt below the *juhgori*. A pair of white *buhsuhn* and *danghye* (silk covered, leather shoes) completed her wedding attire.

Traditionally, when the wedding date was set, the *hahm* was sent to the prospective bride's family from the groom's family. Originally, two rolls of cotton cloth (2 *pil*) for the bride were inside the *hahm*. From around the 16th century, two rolls of red and blue silk, and one silk *joomuhni* (Korean pouch) with 7 grains of red beans as a wish for her to give birth to many sons, were put inside. In later parts of the Yi Dynasty, a male servant in his finery would deliver the *hahm* on his back the night before the wedding. The bride's family would receive it with candle lights at the

Silk *chima* (88 x 112cm) & *juhgori* (21 x 138cm). / 20th c. by Park Sun-young

main, *dae-tchung-maru* (wood floored room), at the center of the house. While this receiving went on, a rowdy neighborhood bunch would sneak in and take away the candles, and return the candles only when they had been treated with wine.

Later in the Yi Dynasty, the groom's best friend conveyed the *hahm*, and the gifts became exorbitantly luxurious items, such as gold from wealthy families. Some young people could not get married, being unable to fulfill the bride's side's expectations. This practice became considered a serious problem and was discussed at the court. They decided to report the list of items, by appointed female inspectors, to check the contents and control expensive gift giving.

The *hahm* was made of fine paulownia wood, which was planted by the parent when the child was born specifically for this purpose. A highly skilled, family retainer craftsman was designated to make the wooden box with metal decorations in auspicious motifs.

In ancient Korea, once the engagement was announced and the wedding date decided, the groom-to-be would come to the bride's house with gifts such as pork, wine, and bundles of money on his back. He would wait outside in front of the gate until the sun set, begging to be let in. Finally, after several requests, the bride's family let him in to his quarter which had been built in the backyard, as if they were doing him a big favor. The wedding ceremony was held at the bride's home on a chosen day. From then on he lived there, helping do all kinds of chores without pay until their first child was born and started to walk. Then he was allowed to take his wife and child to his own home. Koreans describe a man who will be getting married as *Jangga-ganda*,---*Jangga* means bride's home, and *ganda* means going.

Immediately after the wedding, the *pyebaek* (first formal bowing ceremony to her parents-in-law and other close relatives) was held. In earlier times, at the end of the traditional wedding day, the bride and groom retired to their room, and then the bride removed the ceremonial attire, showing her face to the groom for the first time.

Usually, for their first night, a folding screen was provided because inquisitive friends and relatives tried to spy upon them through holes made in the paper windows. On their wedding night, the candle lights were to be extinguished by pinching the wick, or any way other than blowing them out with the mouth. For if they blew the candles out, their good fortune would

Bride & groom's costume designed by Park Sun-young

be blown away like their breath of air. The custom of the groom's stay at the bride's home changed over the years.

The groom would stay at the bride's home for a few days or longer (up to a year), and then the couple moved to the groom's homes. He rode a horse while the bride was carried in a palanquin. As the bride arrived, the *pyebaek* was held to present her to her new family, and offer gifts and food which she had brought from her home.

Her parents-in-law, after receiving her big bow (or prostration), threw jujubes and chestnuts into her *hansam*, as a wish for her to give birth to many sons. Thus, she became a member of her new family, and would not return to her parents' home until the birth of her first child. The *pyebaek* ceremony, and other traditional rituals, are still practiced along with the western style of a white veil and gown, and of course a honeymoon anywhere in the world.

Traditionally, a bride's dowry contained enough *hanbok* to last her lifetime. Great care was taken in choosing the fabric from which *hanbok* was made, because it represented not only the wearer's social status and the wealth of her family, but taste, age, and sex. The number of items and quality also needed to be appropriate for different seasons and occasions.

Today's women generally wear pink *hanbok* or western style dresses for engagement ceremonies. Some hold their wedding ceremonies in two stages; one in western-style wedding gowns, and another in the traditional Korean costume. They change to the traditional red *chima* and green *juhgori* after the wedding for the bowing ceremony, *pyebaek*, to their parents-in-law, and again when paying respect to them upon returning from the honeymoon.

The painstaking effort, not only among older generations, but also among young people, to recreate the details of embroidered costumes for twentieth-century brides indicates the enthusiasm and great affection that they have for their traditional costume, and their intense pride of Korea's cultural heritage.

Sang-bok : Mourning wear

Under strict, Confucian-style mourning, instilling a proper spirit of filial devotion, the sons of a deceased parent were expected to wear humble clothes of rough, undyed hemp. This included a wide-sleeved coat with a somewhat peculiarly designed skirt of three pieces (3 pok) of the same cloth in front, and four pieces in back, over the *juhgori*, *baji*, and leggings, of the same material as *baji*, worn underneath.

A *sam-ttwi* (braided, hemp cord) was tied around the chest.

Commoners' mourning wear

Getting ready for funeral procession of Queen Bangja in 1989 at Kyongbok Palace, Seoul

Queen Soonjong's funeral service, 1966 / Yi Gu's wife, Julia, Bangja, and Yi Gu (R)
Suk Joo-sun Folk Art Museum, Seoul

Prince Yi Gu (Son of Yong-Wang & Bangja) at Queen Bangja's funeral in 1989.

Military bands in yellow uniforms with blue belts and yellow hats

Yi Gu, son of Queen Bangja in *sambae* mourning attire

Tomb of Queen Bangja at Geumgog, Kyonggi Province

A mourner's bamboo staff was carried for the dead father, and a paulownia staff for the dead mother. A *goolkuhn* (high, quadrangular, flat topped, turban-like, hemp headdress) with a head-band of rough hemp cord around the head and a narrow hemp sash, was tied under the chin. Thus, wearing of hemp was closely associated with mourning. Rough cotton *buhsuhn* and *om-shin* (paper covered straw sandals) were worn.

Sang-bok (mournig wear)
19th c.

The married daughter's and the first son's wife, in mourning, also wore rough hemp *chima-juhgori*, and two coats, one over the other, of the same hemp with wide sleeves and a *goreum* tied as a *juhgori*. The outer coat was tied again at the waist with a rough hemp cord. They wore hemp and straw braided head-bands around their heads, or white *jogdoori*, and rough cotton *buhsuhn* and *om-shin*. For unmarried daughters and other daughters-in-law, only one over coat was required, along with a head-band of braided hemp and straw, *buhsuhn*, and *om-shin*.

The *sang-bok*, worn by mourners on the death of their husbands, was made of rough cotton cloth.

Unmarried men, on the other hand, wore a hemp *durumagi*, a hemp belt, a hemp headband, a pair of hemp leggings, and *om-shin*.

In the past, during the 3 years mourning period, the bereaved son had to live plainly in white mourning clothes, with no official duties, music, entertainment, and fine food. With the mortality rate of the time, there must have been many who were in mourning. When a member of royalty passed away, the whole population wore the mourning color of white for three years. For this reason, to many foreign visitors, Korea was a land of white-dressed people.

Suitable clothing was important, even in death, for Koreans, and often their death costumes were prepared while they were still alive. Mourning was such an important and significant part of Korean life that an American doctor, Horace Allen, who worked in Korea in the 1880s and 1890s, wrote that "the dead seem to receive more careful consideration than the living in Korea".

Later, Korean men and women in mourning dressed in subdued or dark colored clothes with arm-bands of ramie fabric for men, and a small white or black bows pinned on their lapel, while women often pinned a white, hemp bow on their hair or a black bow on their blouse or dress, indicating one was in mourning. This is becoming less visible today.

The End of the Yi Dynasty

Since Korea had no relations with the west, western nations called Korea a 'Hermit Kingdom'.

But as western powers gradually entered Asia, Korea could not remain isolated. Eventually, Korea opened the door under pressure at the end of the 19th century, establishing relations with Japan and the west. In 1868, Japan proposed the normalization of relations between Korea and Japan. But the reluctance of Koreans and mishandling by Japanese envoys resulted in another war against Korea in 1870. In addition, there were military threats from France for the execution of a French Catholic priest in 1866, and from the United States for destroying an American merchant ship, the 'General Sherman' on the Dae-dong River near Pyongyang, killing its captain and crew in 1866. The French and Americans invaded Korea and fought a short war on Kanghwa Island, during which time an American, Earnest Oppert, was caught tomb-robbing. This led the Regent Daewon-goon to declare the country officially closed in 1871. But Japan and the western nations did not leave Korea alone. In 1894, the Japanese won a victory in the Sino-Japanese war, and Korea fell to Japanese domination.

The Korean government was forced to sign many agreements with the Japanese, increasing their influence. After the Triple Intervention of Russia, Germany, and France, Japan canceled their lease of the Liaotung peninsula in Manchuria, and while their influence declined, Russian's grew in Korea.

A pro-Russian cabinet replaced the pro-Japanese cabinet. The Russo-Japanese fight over Korea and Manchuria became intense, and Japanese troops invaded Korea again. During this Russo-Japanese War, the Korean government was again forced to sign many agreements with Japan. In the Portmouth Treaty of 1905, which ended the Russo-Japanese War, the Japanese established a protectorate over Korea with the support of Great Britain and the United States, even after Japan and Russia acknowledged Korea's independence.

U.S. president Theodore Roosevelt suggested that Japan put Korea under her control, and even suggested that Japan ought to take over Korea completely. Under these circumstances, the militaristic Japanese threatened and forced the Korean emperor to sign the Treaty of Protection on November 17, 1905. After this, a Japanese

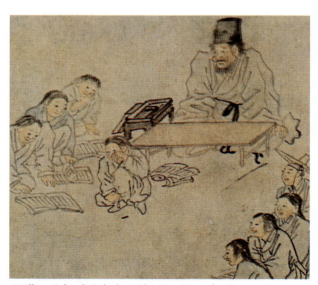

" Village School (*Suh-dang*)" by Kim Hong-do (Danwon)
Genre painting / 18th c.

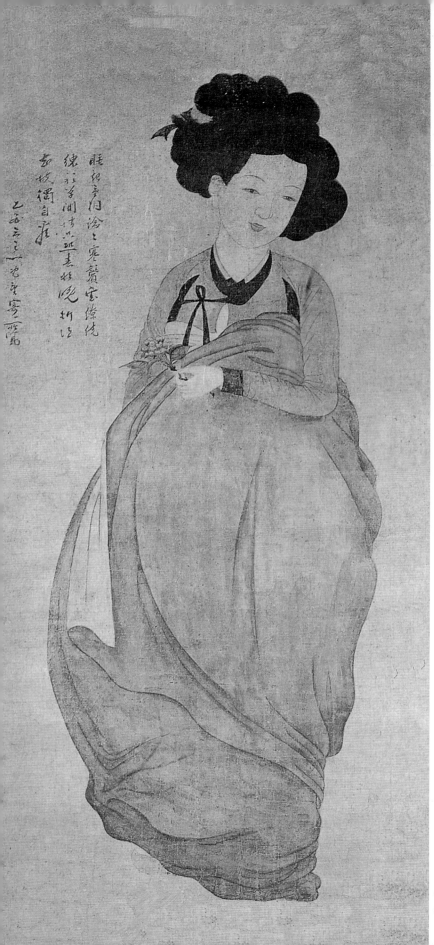

"Beautiful Woman" by Hyewon, Shin Yun-bok
Genre painting / 18th c.

Resident-General was established and ruled Korea, abolishing the Ministry of Foreign Affairs and the Army of Korea. Emperor Gojong's efforts to regain sovereignty and independence were ignored.

The Japanese forced Emperor Gojong to abdicate in July 1907, and Soonjong (first son of Emperor Gojong) was put on the throne as their puppet. After Ito Hirobumi, the first Resident-General, was killed by a Korean patriot, An Chung-geun, in Harbin, Manchuria in 1909, Emperor Soonjong was forced to sign the Treaty of Annexation on August 22, 1910. With this, the Yi Dynasty of 27 rulers and 519 years, ended.

Folk culture began to develop with the deterioration of the 'yangban' dominated society, during and after the Japanese and Manchu wars. Folk arts were very different in subject matter and used decorative bright colors, as well as expressions of freedom and spontaneity, which were not often seen in upper class culture. The Korean genre painters like Kim Hong-do (pen name, Danwon), Shin Yun-bok (Hyewon) and Kim Tuk-shin (Kungjae) of the 18th century, painted fascinating genre paintings of the commoner's daily lives with humor.

Folk songs, dances, narrative music, and musical dramas, developed. Mask dances, puppet shows, and *sijo* (Korean style poetry), became very popular. In addition, *chusa* (a new style of calligraphy) was introduced. The influence of the folk religion, known as 'Shamanism', was evident in folk music and plays. All contributed to the cultural development of the commoners, as well as the upper class of the Yi Dynasty. All of this marvelous art, depicting daily scenes of upper and lower classes in such a whimsical manner at work and play, are valuable sources for custom and costume studies of the era.

5

The Modernization Era

The Modernization Era
(1800 - 1947)

As the western powers built a modern society, after the era of feudalism in the 19th century they did not let Korea remain a secluded nation.

Japanese and western powers pressured Korea to open up and establish modern relations with them. With this open-door policy, Korea faced a variety of problems.

Changes of Men's Clothing

The previous 500 years of Yi Dynasty official attire had been truly complex, distinguishing the high and low, aristocratic and plebeian, and the noble and the mean. With the desire for national independence from Chinese interference, the progressive movement of 1883 was established to modernize the government, promote education, culture, and social progress, including equality. This was the first step toward modernism, and eventually the reform and simplification of official attire was proclaimed by the government.

Durumagi was recommended to become the official or nonofficial ceremonial robe instead of the 'gold crown & court attire' worn before.

In 1883, when the goodwill mission of eleven Koreans arrived in Washington, D.C., the New York Herald described their clothing as consisting of beautiful, purple silk robes, square insignias of embroidered single or

The first Korean goodwill mission Korea sent to America in 1883.

Korean soldiers in western style uniforms.

paired white cranes, snow white trousers, girdles with gold plaques, and hats made of silk and horsehair. This surprised the citizens of Washington and became a conversation piece among the Washington diplomatic community.

All members of the goodwill mission bought a suit of clothes and brought them home, carrying out the costume reform. However, the process of reform among envoys often created a confusing mixture of dress, such as wearing *buhsuhn* with western style leather shoes, and western style hats on top of the *sangtu*.

In 1895, King Gojong (Yi Dynasty) ordered Korean men to cut their hair short and allowed them to wear western style clothes, which created a system of dress. Cutting the *sangtu* off changed the appearance of the whole country over night. There were numerous episodes connected with cutting the hair short, because

King Gojong & Queen Min

according to Confucian beliefs, cutting any part of the body was considered against filial piety. Also because this was forced by the Japanese, anti-pro-Japanese government and anti-Japanese rebelled. However, it was believed to be fitting by progressives to wear short hair with western style clothes, and it appeared to be the first step necessary in becoming a member of the modern world.

Then, late in 1895, the western style uniform was adopted by the military, while horsehair hats, simpler robes, girdles, and mid-calf length boots were appointed for civilian officials. The last big costume design change had occurred when the Chinese 'Tang' style was adopted to be worn with the Korean costume.

Dr. Suh Jae-pil, who studied the democratic form of government and spirit of independence in America, returned to Korea in 1896. In that same year, he established the newspaper called 'Independence Newspaper'. In the editorial section, he strongly advocated the improvement of clothing, food, and shelter, particularly clothing, suggesting that the military, police and other groups of people should be encouraged to wear uniforms with short hair.

Despite the anti-Japanese protestors, because of the conditions of the era, and the conveniences and simplicity of its clothes, it was felt that westernization was necessary. First of all, the government westernized the clothing of envoys, followed by civilian officials, breaking the old system of 500 years of Yi Dynasty official attire.

Civilian officials wore the same uniform as the Japanese ceremonial uniform, which was copied from the British court ceremonial uniform. For minor ceremonies, officials wore the frock coat from Europe and the sack coat from Europe and America.

While many people favored western style clothing and it became very popular, many people still wore Korean traditional costumes in the cities during the 1940s.

In the countryside, particularly, most people preferred the *hanbok*, resisting the new trend.

Juhgori : Jacket

Men's *juhgori*, unlike women's *juhgori* which went through changes of length (short to long and back to short), changed little from the late part of the Yi period. However, the inner-*jucksam* (underwear) were replaced by shirts in the 1920s.

Jokki : Vest

At this time, a new form of *durumagi* (outer robe), *magoja* (outer jacket), and *jokki* (vest) appeared. The *jokki* was an entirely new

Gil Yong-woo in *myungju hanbok* with *jokki* by Hwang Myung-yon

addition to the *hanbok*, and was based on the western style vest, though the originator is not known.

Magoja : Outer coat

The *magoja* was originally worn as an outer jacket by Manchurians. In 1887, when the anti-Chinese ex-Regent Daewon-goon was freed from a Chinese prison (1882-1887), he returned home wearing a *magoja* and it began to spread. It was an outer jacket used in cold weather areas for better warmth. It eventually was worn by women as well.

Jucksam : Unlined summer jacket

The *jucksam* was an unlined, simple, summer jacket made of linen, hemp, or stiffened silk gauze, and worn with *jokki*, which had pockets. It became general wear. Since the summer in Korea is quite hot and humid during the rainy season, the *saeng-mosi* (raw, fine ramie) was ideal for *chima*, *baji*, and *juhgori*. Sometimes *sa* and very fine linen and hemp were also used. The difference between *juhgori* and *jucksam* was that instead of using *goreum* to keep the *juhgori* closed in place, *jucksam* used one button that went through a loop. The

white ramie *jucksam* by Park Sun-young

Kim Eung-suk in silk *magoja* by Jung Sun

button-like knot was made by knotting a narrow, long, folded, and sewed up sash, made of the same material as the jacket, in an intricate manner. The loop was made of the same material as the button, and made by the same narrow folded and sewed up sash. Today, it is still used along with buttons made of amber, gold, silver, or semi-precious stones. There is almost no limit in choosing material for the buttons.

Baji : Trousers

The roomy *baji* remained the same. There were unlined summer *baji* worn with *jucksam*, and made of lighter material, and worn with *sok-baji* (inner *baji*) which was replaced by western style underwear.

Durumagi : Outer robe

The *durumagi* was an outer robe with a gusset which opened only at the front, not like other outer robes from the Yi Dynasty which had openings on both sides, back from a high-waist, and front. It was simple in design and worn by the upper class as everyday wear, and by commoners when they went out. Later, it became general outer wear by all classes. It was outer wear, similar to the western coat, but it was worn throughout the four seasons, even in the hot summer, by using light material, unlike the western coat.

Durumagi worn by men and women by Lee Young-hee

Summer *mosi durumagi* for man

Purple silk *durumagi*

Toshi : Wristlets

Toshi (wristlets) were used for winter and summer. The winter ones were made of silk, cotton, or blended fabrics, and lined for warmth. The summer ones were made of willow branches or horse hair to keep the sleeves free from sweat and for better ventilation. But it lost its use, as the use of shirts, knitted socks, and gloves were introduced in the 1920s.

Buhsuhn: Socks and *shin* : shoes

Even after the knitted *yang-mal* (western style socks) were introduced, *buhsuhn* were necessary. But it was realized that either knitted socks or *buhsuhn* went well with a men's *hanbok*, and people began to wear either one. Shoes were also changed to less expensive rubber shoes in the 1920s. Meanwhile some of the wealthy people began to wear western style leather shoes either with or without shoe laces.

Men's Headdress

Naturally, with the change of hair styles, headdress also changed. By the 1940s, *sangtu* and braided hair were hardly seen anywhere, even in the country. Instead, very close cut, cropped hair and other western styles appeared. Consequently, horse-hair hats disappeared. However, wide-brimmed, straw hats, *sat-gaht*, were still used by farmers in the field to protect them from rain and sun.

Among modernized men, many started to wear western hats with *hanbok* when they went out, and the fashion stayed on. The reason was, when Korea came under oppressive Japanese colonial rule in 1919, and King Gojong abdicated, the whole populace was in sorrow and grief, as if in national mourning. They wore white clothes, but could not find appropriate white *gaht* to wear with the mourning clothes. (All *gaht* makers had been closed since the short-hair order of 1910.) Yet they could not go around bare headed. Luckily, just in time, there were hat makers who sold hats that looked much like the white *gaht*, panama hats.

Panama hats and straw hats, were made by South Americans, Equadorians and Southeast Asians, not by the Japanese. Those hats remained popular and stayed on to be worn with men's *hanbok*. When the clever Japanese noticed the high demand

Gentleman in panama hat with *Hanbok* 20th c.

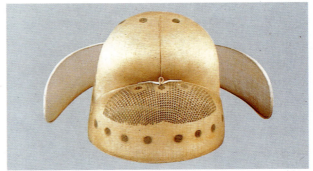

Baeksa-mo (white *sa-mo*) worn during the mourning by officials in Yi Dynasty

and low supply of panama and straw hats, they made excess profits by making and selling felt hats.

The cold weather hat, *nambawi* continued for a while among country elderly people.

⬤ *Gomooshin* (rubber Shoes)

People around 50 years old or older can remember wearing Korean rubber shoes. Around 1921, shoes made of leather, or with hemp upper parts and rubber soles, were introduced from Kobe, Japan. These were called 'economical shoes' or 'convenient shoes'. Originally, Americans had the idea of rubber rain shoes when they saw how South American Indian tribes extracted sap from rubber plants and applied them thickly onto the bottom of their feet for protection.

By 1932, the supple rubber shoes in Indian Canoe-shapes had been produced for the first time in Korea. The brand name was *Kyong*, the first Chinese character of the manufacturer's name, *Kyong-sung-gomu*. They became quite popular as they were very practical for farming during the long rainy season. They became so popular that people wore them everyday in many different colors for women and in black or white for men, and even for children.

White rubber shoes.

Contemporary leather shoes in same shape as rubber shoes

Man wearing rubber shoes

Model Ringe wearing silk *hanbok* by Lee Hyo-jae & *gomooshin*

Change of Women's Clothing & Accessories

After the treaties with Japan and the United States, the Korean government sent missions to Japan in 1881, and to the U.S. in 1883, to learn more about these countries and promote friendship. The members of the missions were awestruck and impressed by these countries' advances and strengths, and they felt the urgency for Korea to change and modernize its system.

The arrival of the Christian belief, in 1885, of 'all men being created equal under God' attracted many women, and encouraged equality for women, influencing spiritual modernism. After *Gapsin Juhngbyuhn* (a coup d'etat carried out by the Progressives against Chinese intervention in Korean internal affairs in 1884), missionaries established religious freedom, and contributed in the fields of education and social organization, spreading and influencing modernism rapidly. In a true sense, Korean women's freedom was born by the introduction of Christianity. Korean women came out of the secluded inner-court to get an education. It was an extremely difficult task for missionaries to convince Korean society of the importance of education for women. But, slowly, women began to participate in social activities, were educated with men, and even went abroad for further studies.

Missionaries taught the concept of freedom, rights, and equality, as new cultural trends developed.

At the same time in 1896, when Dr. Suh Jae-pil returned from 10 years of exile in America after *Gapsin Juhngbyuhn*, he encouraged women to realize the value of education, and participate in politics and independence movements. Women became now free to choose to love and marry, and divorce, which was truly an awesome change.

Along with women's social activities, women's costume required changes from the traditional Korean costume to a simpler and convenient western style. The western missionary women were certainly a great influence. But instead of wearing the western style clothing directly, they made the Korean jacket longer and the skirt shorter, for better mobility when they went out. (They still wore long skirts at home.) It was viewed as a wonderful change, and

A student in bloomer, designed by missionary teachers for Ewha Gymn. class / 1927. Ewha Womans Univ. Archives, Seoul

Students at Gymn class in *Tong-chima* and missionary teacher, Miss Walter. 1910./ Ewha Womans Univ. Archives, Seoul

the number of women adopting this fashion increased.

Western style dress was first worn in 1899 by Yun Ko-ra. This was very conspicuous to general Koreans, and became a conversation topic. In 1900 Esther Park returned from Baltimore in elegant western dress after studying medicine for four years, becoming the first woman medical doctor in Korea.

Gradually, western style clothing became fashionable. Notably, the Japanese style was worn only by a limited number of women because of anti-Japanese feelings.

However, hair styles, underwear, slips, socks, and shoes were the same as before. Still, Choi Hwa-ran returned from Tokyo with a pompadour hair style, in western stockings, and western style leather shoes, and a black *tong-chima* (short skirt) in 1907 which created much talk about town, way before the word "modern girl" came out.

Five years before Korean liberation, in August 15, 1945, during the national suffering period of the Japanese occupation, Koreans' clothing had to go through many ordeals. The Japanese forced Korean men to wear "*Gookminbok*", a kind of uniform, and women to wear shapeless slacks (called "*mompae*"), absurd looking pants worn by Japanese female laborers.

Tong chima worn by Miss Conrow's Ewha students
1941
Ewha Womans University Archives, Seoul

Women's Headdress

While the country was in the process of modernization, there were still court ceremonies and upper class laws and regulations. However, after the end of the Yi Dynasty, court ceremonies were no longer necessary and ceremonial dress became a relic of the past.

For a while most women kept the old hair styles, braided hair with ribbons for unmarried girls, and chignons for married ladies. The custom of wearing wigs had not disappeared completely either. Since there was not much that they could do about changing clothing without being too conspicuous, modern women turned more attention to their hair styles and shoes.

By the 1920s, the first beautician, who was trained in Japan, opened a beauty salon at Whashin department store. There was conventional braided hair for younger girls. For older girls the style was braids, folded up two or three times, and attached on the back of the head with a butterfly style ribbon. Another style was hair piled up on top of the head, made into a bun, and secured with a ribbon. Some women even braided their hair and put it around the head like a turban.

After 1930, long braided hair disappeared, except on the country side. For suddenly, by 1934, the short hair style was sweeping Korea. By 1937 the permanent wave had arrived on the scene. Every modern girl cut her hair short and curled it.

As hair styles changed, hair accessories such as *ttuljam* and *chuhpji* disappeared along with big wigs, and the luxurious crossbar and hairpins became simpler. The large crossbar and hairpins that decorated the bun were used only for wedding ceremonies, and became family heirlooms.

Hats such as *jobawi* and *nambawi* were still seen up to 1930. The *jogdoori* (crown) is still worn by brides for traditional wedding ceremonies. The *nuhwool* or *jang-ot* were gone long before the 1930s, when women came out of seclusion and the custom of separating males and females ended. It was replaced by the parasol.

Parasol shading two ladies.

A class room of Ewha Girls' School.
Ewha Womans Univ. Archives, Seoul

Ewha students with traditional hair styles
1920s
Ewha Womans Univ. Archives, Seoul

Ewha students with different hair styles
1920s - 1930s
Ewha Womans Univ. Archives, Seoul

6
Contemporary Creations

Contemporary Creations
(1948-the Present)

In the twentieth century, Korean clothing has undergone many changes. No longer is there control of costume design and decoration, once of vital importance to the imperial system. No longer are there sumptuary laws and costume regulations, which were recurring themes in dynastic history. Women no longer weave their own fabrics or sew their own clothing. Chemical dyes and bolts of man-made fabrics have reached all sectors of society. Today, in the cities of industrialized Korea, more practical, western-style clothing is favored for normal working days.

However, the *hanbok* has not only survived, but its revival is sweeping the nation along with economic prosperity and national pride. In affluent contemporary Korea, more and more people prefer *hanbok* for formal or festive occasions such as wedding ceremonies, New Year's Day, or the Full Moon Festival. It is an exciting and breathtaking renaissance. As the general population becomes wealthier and living standards rise, people are demanding more elaborate clothing with more luxurious fabrics and designs. The wealthy in the cities want to live well and enjoy the good things in life, and they want fine traditional Korean clothing. To meet the demand, a variety of rich *hanbok*, combining age old techniques with contemporary sensitivity, have been created in recent years by weavers, dyers, embroiderers, designers, painters, seamstresses, and gold and silver leaf imprinters.

Although there is only the one basic dress design, using the body's shape as the basis for collars, lapels, sleeves, trouser legs, and bodices, every dress looks different. One may see a long, billowing, full skirt or roomy *baji* of one color, and a short jacket of another or the same color. The unlimited color combinations can be unexpected and exquisite, serene and elegant, and bold. Colors vary from all white with a black belt, pink and silver grey, blue and eggplant purple, yellow, grey and rose, lavender and sea green, lime green and brown, and multi-colored flowers worn with silent, supple, rubber shoes or leather shoes. In the summer, the parasols play an important part in Korean women's ensembles.

Young couple in *hanbok* walking at the old palace

Choi Sun & Park Sung-yong in silk *durumagi* by Lee Na-kyong

Chima & *juhgori* in contemporary color combinations by Park Sun-young

Young bride in modernized wedding attire

Author's son & his bride dancing in formal wedding attire at their wedding reception

Choi Sun in *no-bang* (Spring & Autumn) *hanbok* by Lee Na-kyong

Yim Ji-eun & Lee Bum-suk in silk *hanbok* by Lee Jin

Jo Min-soo and a girl in *myun* (cotton) & boy in *ma* (hemp) *hanbok* by Lee Na-kyong

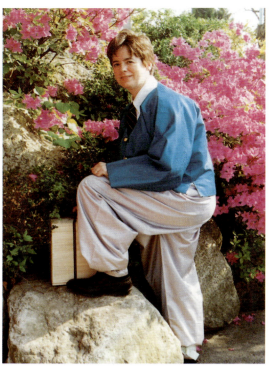

R. J. in silk brocade *magoja* & silk satin *baj* with western style shirts, tie, socks, and shoes
S. Yang Collection

Pat Lucas in contemporary silk *durumagi* over *chima* & *juhgori*
Suh Mi-kyong collection
1996

Hyoongbae on western style dress
Embroidered by Rita Rikken Jansen

Wall hanging embroidered by Karen Boyette

Joomuhni embroidered by Rita Rikken Janssen

Park Sun-young, designated as Intangible Cultural Asset #11 by the government in 1996, has been designing and sewing *hanbok*, which she learned from her mother, for over 48 years. Her delicate and elegant *hanbok* creations for her customers, which

Park Sun-young with her students

she also wears, are soft spoken, petite, and delicate, like herself. Her shop in Ewha-dong, Jongro-gu, Seoul, is simple and comparably small for her fame, yet serene and comfortable. It is filled with beautiful silk fabric and clothing she has made, and which have received awards. She bases her designs and methods of sewing *hanbok* on traditional techniques, continues to do research, participate in exhibitions, and teaches young people to carry on the tradition.

Mosi jucksam & chima

Park Sun-young designed this costume in commemoration of 1988 Seoul Olympic Games

Wedding attire

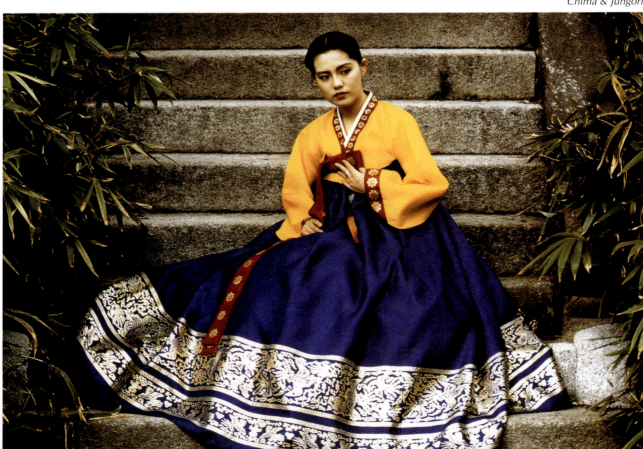

Chima & juhgori

Chang Yeun-soon, a fiber artist, patch-worked Korean traditional cloths, hemp, and wisteria vines to create an installation art for exhibition at the Walker Hill Art Center in 1996. Using hemp, a dominary element of Korean clothing for hundreds of years, she searched for the meaning of beauty, life, truth, and wisdom in a square room.

" Sudden shaking off the dust of mind... ".
Hemp and wisteria vines.
85 x 85 x 170cm.
1996.

" The wind blowing in at the bosom of the elite *Wha Rang* ".
Hemp and wisteria vines. / 80 x 100cm. / 1995.

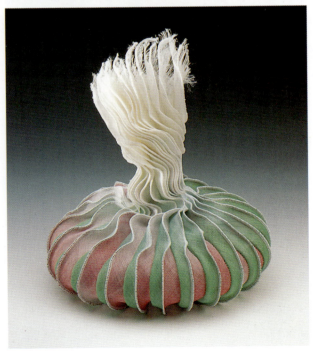

" Feeling of Fabric ".
Hemp. / 17.5 x 17.5 x 20cm. / 1987.

Jilkyong-ee Woori-ot (plantain our clothing), a brand name, uses natural dyes that Korean ancestors used. Lee Ki-yeun, head of *Jilkyong-ee*, obtains natural dyes from the plants she cultivated, which is extremely time and effort consuming, but she believes it a worthwhile task, creating beautiful end results. The modified designs of Korean clothing in subdued natural colors and simpler practical styles, using traditional knotted buttons and loops instead of tie-ribbons, have become very popular because they are comfortable and easy to care for in contemporary life styles. Shoes are also made in a traditional style with contemporary materials, which go very well with these clothes.

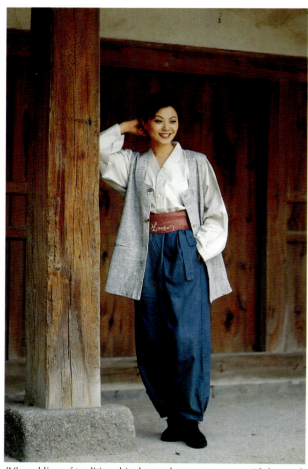

'V' neckline of traditional jacket and roomy trouser with knotted buttons at ankles instead of *denim* (sash)
White *juhgori*, gray outer jacket, and blue trouser with brick red waistband.

Men in 'V' neckline jacket, olive color vest, and brick red trouser.

Modified versrion of Korean leather shoes

Hanbok designers suggest using more subdued and quiet colors and motifs for contemporary *hanbok* to last longer. Since traditional Korean costumes used two distinctive colors for *juhgori-chima* and *baji*, they consider good color combinations to be very important. For women they favor jujube colored skirts and red bean-pink or pale yellow jackets, dark-mugwort green skirts and gingko-light green jackets, and mid-pink skirts and pale pink jackets for younger women.

Also, for men, they prefer neutral colors such as *ok-saek* (pale-jade-green) and pigeon or silver-gray are suggested. They emphasize the importance of undergarments. The slip should be always 2-3 cm. shorter than the skirt so that it will not show. For men, trousers should be tied one-fold leftward at the waist and tied by a sash (*ttwi*).

At the ankle one-fold should be taken inward at the outside, above the *buhsuhn* (cotton socks), and tied by a *daenim* (small sash), which should go around the ankle twice, about 3 cm. above the hem. Regarding *goreum* for *juhgori*, one should be about 2 cm. longer than the other for better balance after being tied. For both men and women, white *buhsuhn* and commonly worn supple rubber shoes are proper. But when it is necessary to wear leather shoes, women look better in white low-heeled shoes, and men look better in white western style socks with black shoes. When going out, *durumagi* (outer robes) should be worn by both men and women for appropriateness.

With the stresses of modern life, clothing that is simple, uncomplicated, and comfortable, can make people feel better. The design of the *Hanbok* certainly provides that comfort, and the textile and fashion industries, with a new spirit in the air, are making advances based on innovations of their own and from abroad. With their beauty and value in mind, talented and resourceful artisans continue creating with the spirit of traditional arts and crafts, and pride in their country's cultural heritage. This stimulates interest in revitalizing traditional costumes and techniques from the past into the mainstream of Korean life. Hopefully this will encourage more people to find new ways of applying the traditions of old towards modern creations.

Hwang Hye-bong, a fifth generation Korean traditional silk covered leather shoe-maker, lives and works in Karak-dong, Songpa-gu, Seoul. His great-great grand father and great-grand father were Yi Dynasty royal court shoe-makers and made *jucksuk* (red silk covered formal shoes) for King Gojong. *Got-shin* (flower embroidered silk shoes) worn by the late wife of former president Park Chung-hee were made by his grand father, who was designated as Important Intangible Cultural Asset #37.

He decided to carry on the family profession when he saw his 86 year old grand father teaching the technique of shoe making to his 64 year old father. He has been making shoes for 20 years.

Got-shin by Hwang Hye-bong

When he started, the *got-shin*, worn by the upper class, was losing popularity because of rubber shoes made during the Japanese occupation period (1920s-1930s) and by spread of western style leather shoes.

To complete a pair of silk covered shoes 72 steps are required. It begins with cutting layered mulberry paper, then cutting, pressing, and folding white leather for the sole. Later, ten longevity symbols or flower motifs were embroidered on silk damask. Then, embroidered silk was glued on, using a wooden shoe form. The end result is an art piece.

It takes about 2 weeks to make a pair. It is hard and time consuming work. Because Hwang Hye-bong believes that someone has to carry on the tradition, his work continues with spirit put into the *got-shin*, recreating shoes worn by kings, queens, and *Gisaeng*.

Choi Bok-hee (67), a seamstress at the *Hangook judan* (silk goods store for custom made Korean costumes), recreated 50 pieces of Yi Dynasty court costumes in her spare time with her own savings. She saved up money from her regular salary, and staying up until very late each night, she averaged 2 to 3 hours of work on the pieces a day for almost 3 years.

The collection includes the green *dang-ui* of the three or four year old princess Duk-hye, the only daughter of King Gojong, and a red skirt with gold-leaf imprint, *Heuk-yongpo* (every day wear for an adult prince), a red armor with 700 round brass studs, worn by King Soonjong, etc. Ever since she started working at the silk goods store in Jong-ro, 43 years ago, she collected the materials thinking she may need them in the future. Her collection shows her special affection toward Korean costume, and superior sewing skill, which is unsurpassed by the machine.

She did the dyeing herself if she did not have or could not find the right colored material. Her *ondol* floor was ruined while working on the armor. She read many books and visited museums for better information.

She not only recreated these pieces, but also donated the entire set to the National Museum in Duksoo Palace.

Certainly her contribution will remain an important and valuable source for Korean traditional costume studies, and is greatly appreciated by all who have interest in Korean culture and costume.

Reproduction of *sakyu-sam* & *hwal-ot* by Choi Bok-hee

Sul Yoon-hyung, a fashion designer, creates stunning western style dresses accentuated with a Korean traditional flair, such as *goreum* used as a long sash tied around waist, *jogagbo* (patch work wrappers) used as a wide sash or a part of the skirt, *joomuhni* enlarged as back packs to be worn with black dresses, or airy, colorful, summer dresses made of hemp or ramie patch work. Sophisticated dresses with exotic Korean motifs are the mark of her creations.

Modified version of *jobawi*, *toshi* & embroidered bodice of beautiful silk dress

197

Myungju (silk) dress with patchwork

Big colorful pouch turned to a back pack

Silk *jobawi* & enl
spoon case as acce

198

Bright ramie patchwork dress

199

Myun (cotton) beach wear modified from *hanbok chima*

Myungju (silk) vest, blouse & trousers

Jogagbo (*mosi* patchwork) to wear as lap-around skirt

Multi-colored *mosi jogagbo* (ramie patchwork) dress for summer

201

Huh Young, a traditional Korean dress designer, reproduces the characteristics of traditional dress in flowing lines and profound colors. His brilliant choice and combinations of colors balances and complements the wearers' individual shape. His exquisite dolls in traditional Korean costumes have been exhibited in many cities.

Some of Huh Young's magnificent costume recreated and shown at fashion show held in Washington, D. C.

Great ceremonial attire for empress

Offering (*Myungju* robe)

Sookgosa nok-wonsam for bride. & *hwal-ot* for *pyebaek* ceremony. / 20th c.

On the whole, Koreans are more interested in what they wear and more concerned about their appearance than many other people. The reason is rooted in the country's long aristocratic period of the Yi Dynasty, in which wearing distinctive apparel was closely related to social status and occupation. Wearing the right clothing went beyond just importance. No commoner dared to attempt to dress up as a scholar-official, for example, putting his life and the security of his family in jeopardy. This compelling concern for appearance has carried over into modern times and made Koreans particularly conscious not only of style, but of name brands as well.

On the other hand, Koreans have learned through the mystical doctrines of Buddhism and the classics of Confucianism that a man should not be ashamed of coarse food, humble clothing, or a modest dwelling, but should only be ashamed of not being cultivated in the perception of 'beauty'. A man has no place in society unless he understands aesthetics. The end of the twentieth century finds Koreans continuing the search for the true meaning of beauty in the world through *Hanbok*.

Bibliography

Adams, Edward B. *Korean Folk Art and Craft.* Seoul International Publ. House, 1987.

Adams, Edward B. *Korea's Pottery Heritage.* Seoul International Publ. House, Vol. I, 1986, Vol. II. 1990.

Allen, Horace N. *Things Korean.* 1908. RAS-KB Reprint, 1980.

The Art of Kim, Hong-do, the special exhibition catalogue commemorating his 250th anniversary. National Museum, Seoul, 1995.

Bishop, Isabella Bird. *Korea and Her Neighbors.* Yonsei U. P., 1980.

Bunge, Frederica M., ed. *South Korea*: Washington: U.S. Government Printing Office, 1987.

Cho, Hyo-soon. *Bokshik.* Daewonsa, Seoul, 1990.

Covell, Jon Carter. *Japan's Hidden History: Korean Impact on Japanese Culture.* Hollym, Seoul, 1984.

Covell, Jon Carter. *Korea's Cultural Roots*, Hollym, Seoul, 1981, 1982, 1992.

Crane, Paul. *Korean Patterns.* Seoul: Royal Asiatic Society, Korea Branch, 1978.

Garrett, Valery M. *Chinese Clothing: An Illustrated Guide.* Oxford U.P., Oxford New York, 1994.

Goepper, Roger & Whitfield, Rodrick. *Treasures From Korea.* British Museum Publications, London, England, 1987.

Han, Suzanne Crowder. *Notes on Things Korean.* Hollym, Seoul, 1995.

Han, Young-hwa. *Juntong Jasoo (Traditional Embroidery).* Daewonsa, Seoul, 1990.

Henderson, Gregory. *Korea: The Politics of the Vortex.* Cambridge, Ma: Harvard U. P., 1968.
Hulbert, Homer B. *The Passing of Korea.* New York: Doubleday, reprinted by Yonsei U. P., Seoul, 1969.

Huh, Dong-hwa. *Crafts of the Inner Court: The Artistry of Korean Women.* The Museum of Korean Embroidery, 1987.

Hyun, Peter, ed.. *Introducing Korea.* Jungwoo-sa, Seoul, 1979, 1987.

Janelli, Roger L., & Janelli, Dawnhee. *Ancestor Worship and Korean Society.* Stanford U.P., 1982.

Kang, he-won. *The Evaluation of National Costume of Korean Womem.* (Masters Thesis) Univ. of Maryland, 1964.

Kendall, Laurel & Griffin Dix., eds. *Religion and Ritual in Korean Society.* Institute of East Asian Studies, U. of California., 1987.

Kim, Chewon & Lena Kim Lee. *Arts of Korea.* Tokyo, Kodansha International, 1973.

Kim, H. Edward. *Korea Beyond the Hills.* Eul-Yoo, Seoul, 1987 (reprint).

Kim, H. Edward. *The Korean Smile.* Hollym, Seoul, 1990.

Kim, Han-kyo. *Studies on Korea: A Scholar's Guide.* Honolulu: U. P. of Hawaii, 1980.

Kim, Richard. *The Martyred.* Si-sa-o-sa, Seoul, 1962.

Kim, Won-yong. *Art and Archaeology of Ancient Korea.* Taekwang, Seoul, 1986.

Kim, Yong-suk & Son, Kyong-ja. *An Illustrated History of Korean Costume*, Vol. I & II, Yekyong, Seoul, 1984.

The Korea Overseas Information Service. *Facts about Korea.* Hollym, Seoul, 1986.
The Korea Overseas Information Service. *Korean Art Guide.* 2nd ed., Yekyong, Seoul, 1987.

Ku, Dae-yeol. *Korea Under Colonialism: The March First Movement and Anglo-Japanese Relations.* RAS-KB, Seoul, 1985.

Kwon, Yoon-hee (Suk). *Symbolic and Decorative Motifs of Korean Silk*: 1875-1975. Ilji-sa, Seoul, 1988.

Ledyard, Gari. *The Dutch Come to Korea.* RAS-KB, Seoul, 1971.

Lee, Ki-baik. *A New History of Korea.* Translated by Edward W. Wagner with Edward J. Shultz. Cambridge, MA: Harvard U. P., 1984.

Lee, O-young, trns. by Holstein, John. *Korea in Its Creations.* Design House, Seoul, 1994.

Lee, Sun-ok & McCurdy, John Chang. *Zen Dance: Meditation in Movement.* Seoul International Publ. House, 1985.

Marcus, Richard, ed.. *Korean Studies Guide.* Berkely: U. Cal. P., 1954.

The Museum of Korean Embroidery. *The Special Embroidery Exhibition of Chosun Dynasty.* Seoul, 1988.

Nam, Andrew C.. *A Panorama of 5000 Years: Korean History.* Hollym, Seoul, 1988.

A Photographic Look at the Chosun Dynasty. So Mun Dang, Seoul, 1987. Yi Dynasty Through Pictures (Life and Customs).

Rutt, Richard. *Korean Works and Days: Notes from the diary of a Country Priest.* Seoul: Royal Asiatic Society, Korea Branch, 1964, reprinted 1978.

Solberg, S. E.. *The Land and People of Korea.* Harper Collins, New York, 1991.

Suk, Joo-sun. *Hankook Bokshik Sa (History of Korean Costumes).* BoJin Jae, Seoul, 1971, 1st. ed. 5th reprinted, 1992.

Suk, Joo-sun. *Hioong-bae* (Insignia Patterns in Yi Dynasty). Folk Art Research Collection Series I. The Suk Joo-sun Memorial Museum of Korean Folk Arts, Dankook Univ., Seoul, 1979.
Jang-shin-koo (Personal Ornaments in Yi Dynasty). Series II, 1981.
Ui (Clothes of Yi Dynasty). Series III, 1985.
Gwan-mo & Soo-shik (Ornated Korean Traditional Hats). Series, IV, 1993.

Won, Yong-chol. *Korean Culture.* Vol. 12, No. 4, periodical Los Angeles, 1991.

Yang, Sunny & Narasin, Rochelle M. *Textile Art of Japan.* Shufunotomo, Tokyo, 1989.

Yoo, Hye-kyoung, *Hankook Bokshicksa Youn-gu* (Korean Costume History Study), Ewha Woman's Univ. Press, 1980.

Zhou, Xun & Gao, Chunming. *5000 Years of Chinese Costumes.* Eng. ed. by China Books & Periodicals, San Francisco, 1987.

Zozayong, ed., *The Life of Buddha in Korean Painting.* Joint RAS-KB/ Emileh Museum Publ., Seoul, 1975.

Sources

AGABANG Co., LTD.
678-36 Youksam-dong
Gangnam-gu, Seoul
Tel (02) 527-1340~4
Fax (02) 553-5365

Karen Boyette (Embroiderer)
11-412, Hannam-dong
Yongsan-gu, Seoul
Tel (02) 796-0096

Chang Youn-soon (Fiber Artist)
Prof. Ewha Womans University
11-1 Daehyon-dong
Suhdaemoon-gu, Seoul
Tel (02) 3216-8451

Choi Bok-hee (Hanbok Designer & Seamstress)
Hangook Joodan
102-1 Jongro 2-ga
Jongro-gu, Seoul
Tel (02) 733-6164, 4091   386-1198

Chosun Ilbo (Chosun Daily Newspaper)
61 Taepyongro 1-ga
Jung-gu, Seoul
Tel (02) 724-5114

Chung Hee-sook (Editor)
Areum-dawn Wuri-ot (Monthly Magazine)
82 Bomun-dong 4 ga
Suhngbook-gu, Seoul
Tel (02) 927-1420~1   923-5923
Fax (02) 927-1125

Design House publishers, Inc.
186-210 Jangchung-dong 2 ga
Jung-gu, Seoul 100-392, Korea
Tel (02) 275-6151
Fax (02) 275-7884

Ewha Womans University Archives & Museum
11-1 Daehyon-dong
Suhdaemoon-gu, Seoul
Tel (02) 360-3152
Fax (02) 360-3153

Gallery Mook
1-97, Dongsoong-dong
Jongro-gu, Seoul 110-510, Korea
Tel (02) 745-2980
Fax (02) 744-2329

Huh Young (Hanbok Designer)
Huh Young Hanbok (Fabrics & Custom Clothes)
62-35 Tchuhngdam-dong
Gangnam-gu, Seoul
Tel (02) 542-7677~9

IBM Korea, Inc.
25-11 Yoido-dong
Yeongdeungpo-gu, Seoul, Korea
Tel (02) 781-6921
Fax (02) 782-2755

Rita Rikken Janssen (Embroiderer)
657-123, Hannam-dong
Yongsan-gu, Seoul
Tel (02) 792-5932

Kim Duk-whan (Gold-leaf Imprinter)
237-16 Jungja-dong
Boondang-gu, Sungnam-shi
Kyounggi-do, Korea
Tel (0342) 713-2067

King Sejong University Museum
98 Gunja-dong
Gwangjin-gu, Seoul
Tel (02) 460-0076

Korea University Museum
1 Anam-dong 5 ga
Suhngbook-gu, Seoul
Tel (02) 953-1528, 926-4381

Kyongju National Museum
76 Inwang-dong
Kyongju-si, Kyongsangbook-do, Korea
Tel (0561) 772-5193

Lee Hyo-jae (Hanbok designer)
Ewha Ot-bang (fabrics & custom clothes)
347-32 Ahyun-2 dong
Mapo-gu, Seoul
Tel (02) 393-4766   362-1490

Lee Young-hee (Hanbok Designer)
665-5 Shinsa-dong
Gangnam-gu, Seoul
Tel (02) 545-0689, 544-0630, 543-0227
Fax (02) 517-3534

109 Rie Di Bac, 75007
Paris, France
Tel 42 84 24 84
Fax 42 84 18 59

National Folklore Museum
1 Sejongro
Jongro-gu, Seoul
Tel (02) 734-1346, 720-3136

National Museum
1-57 Sejongro
Jongro-gu, Seoul
Tel (02) 398-5000

Onyang Folk Art Museum
403-1 Gwongok-dong
Asan-si, Chungchongnam-do, Korea
Tel (0418) 42-6001~4

Park Sun-young (Hanbok Desinger)
Intangible Cultural Asset #11
98-4 Ewha-dong
Jongro-gu, Seoul
Tel (02) 742-2438   766-0463

Park Yuhn-ok (Water-color Artist)
Meein-do (Beautiful Woman)
400-4 Changshin-dong
Samil APT 5-609
Jongro-gu, Seoul
Tel (02) 231-4129

PRO WORK STUDIO
Ga-yong Bldg.
689 Yuhgsam-dong
Gangnam-gu, Seoul
Tel (02) 554-1236

The Suk Joo-sun Memorial Museum of Korean
    Folk Arts, Dankook University
8 Hannam-dong
Yongsan-gu, Seoul
Tel (02) 709-2188

Sul Yun-hyong (Fashion Designer)
Sul Yun-hyong Boutique
62-39 Tchuhngdam-dong
Gangnam-gu, Seoul
Tel (02) 512-3384~5

Traditional Cultural Photo. Research Center
52-2 Tchoongmooro, 2-ga, #306
Joong-gu, Seoul
Tel (02) 277-2599

WELCOME Advertising
31-5 Jangchoon-dong 1 ga
Dugyang Bldg. 6th Fl.
Joong-gu, Seoul
Tel (02) 274-4636
Fax (02) 278-0140

Yim Min-ye (Hanbok Designer)
Korean Folk Costume
34-149 Itaewon-dong
Yongsan-gu, Seoul
Tel (02) 793-5420~1

Index

Amnok River 30
an-bang 79
anchae 79
An Chung-geun 168
andong-po 37
an-sarang 79
badook 78
baeja 128
baekmal 142
baeksaek-hwa 32
baenae-juhgori 152
baji 18, 22, 28, 127, 128, 174
Banja 69, 71
bang-shim-gokryong 81
bangsuhk 20
bichwi-dae 62
bichwi-gae 123
binyuh 43, 104, 116
bo 65, 76
bojagi 60
bok 100
bokkuhn 84, 152
bok-tu 51
bong-jam 71, 99
boonjae 79
boryo 78
buhsuhn 26, 47, 91, 104, 177
buhsuhn-jang 92
chaek 28
chaekgori 78
cha-il 60
Changdok Palace 96
chilbo-hwakwan 104
chima 22
chohye 18, 87
chuhn-min 54
chuhpji 181
chusa 168
Crown Prince 75, 76, 100
dae 26, 32
daenggi 30, 43, 159
daenim 33, 195
Daewon-goon 94, 128
dal 142
dan 42, 152
dangcho muni 30
danghye 103, 136, 159
dang-ui 76, 103, 196
dan-sok-ot 60, 130
dari-sok-ot 130
dongjuhng 56, 84, 140

dopo 49, 86
dorong-ee 138
dotjari 60
doturak-daenggi 109, 159
Duksoo Palace 69, 76, 196
durumagi 28, 49, 174, 195
dwitkkoji 59, 116
ee 18
eebul 20, 49
eun-jangdo 117
gachae 71, 99, 102, 113
gachi durumagi 152
gaht 31, 87
gajook-mituri 91
Gakjuh-chong 28, 132
gang-po 37
gangsapo 66
gapju 139
gap-sa 39
Gapsin Juhngbyuhn 179
gasa 140
geisha 150
geum-bak-pan 110
geum-gwan 32, 80, 87
geumjik-daenggi 71
geumsu-ojo-yong-bo 76
gisaeng 54, 146
git 56
giyut-magi 57
gojaeng-ee 60
Gojong, King 69, 83, 87, 94, 168,
    171, 177, 195
gokkal 142
gomooshin 178
gong-dan 42
gong-jung-chaek 65
Gongmin, King 51, 62, 64
gon-yongpo 65
Gookminbok 180
goolkuhn 166
goonggo 22
goot 151
goreum 43, 57, 81
got-shin 195
guhn 48
guhngwik 32
gujangbok 62, 96
Guknaesong 26
gwan 113
gwan-dae 156
Gwanghaegun 113

gwanggo 22
hae 142
haengjon 142
hahm 159
hak 84
hakchang-ui 85
Hangeul 55
hang-ra 39, 80
hansam 102, 106, 149
hapi 99
heuk-hwa 91
heuk-hye 84
heukjangsam 140
heuk-ui 136
heuk-yongpo 75, 196
hol 62
holtae 28
hong-po 76
hong-yongpo 66
hoo-seul 99
hoosoo 63, 79
hwa 18, 26, 32, 39, 48
hwa-gwan 99
hwal-ot 105
hwamunsa 39, 100
hwang-wonsam 76
hwang-yongpo 64
hwaro 78
hwiho 60
hyoongbae 78, 92
hyoong-dae 66
icksungwan 65, 75
Imhasilgi 113
Ito Hirobumi 168
jajuk-yongpo 65, 71, 75
jambang-ee 28
jang-ot 60, 133
jangsado 29
jangshingu 130
Jinduck, Queen 22
Jin-Wangja 71, 76
jipshin 134
jobawi 115, 152
jobok 66, 79
jogagbo 197
jogdoori 47, 105, 113
jok 30, 116, 159
jokki 120, 172
Jongmyo 51, 63, 81
joomuhni 120, 159, 197
joongchimak 87

joong-dan 63, 66
joong-in 54
jucksam 173
jucksuk 48, 64, 195
juhgori 22, 71, 96, 127, 172
juhkpi-hwa 32
juhnbok 87, 152
juhndae 139
julpoong-mo 32
Jumansik 143
jungja-gwan 87
jyebok 81
jye-gwan 81
Koguryo Kingdom, The 26
Koryo History 64
Koryo Kingdom, The 46
Kyongbok Palace 157, 158
kyong-dae 123
Kyong-sung-gomu 178
ma 26
maedeup 120
magoja 128, 173
Manchuria 29, 30
mangguhn 31, 88
man-ja 43, 80
mareun-shin 103
mituri 134
mobon-dan 42
Modernization Era, The 170
moja 88
mok-hwa 65
mok-shin 136
mok-tak 142
mompae 180
moo 129
mosi 18, 38, 84
mudang 150
muhri-suguhn 132
munyo-bok 151
muri-kkoji 116
Muryong, King 34
myun 48
myun-bok 62, 63
myungju 18, 40, 127
myunyugwan 63, 66
nae-ui 130
nambawi 113
namu-shin 136
nokpihye 84
nok-wonsam 100, 159
norigae 59, 71, 117
nuhwool 48, 112
obang-haeng 152

obang-nang-ja 123
obang-wi 152
o-hyuk-ee 34
ok 118
okdae 63, 65
ok-gyu 63
ok-hol 66
ok-saek 195
Old Shilla Kingdom, The 22
om-shin 166
ondol-bang 20
opi-hwa 32
O-un-taepyung-song 23
Paekche Kingdom, The 33
pi-gap 139
pyebaek 105, 160
pyeseul 63, 96
ra 39
sa 39
sabang-gwan 87
saektong 102
saektong juhgori 152
saenggosa 39
saeng-mosi 173
sakyu-sam 71, 76
sambae 37
Samgook Sagi 22, 33, 46
Samgook Yusa 22, 47
samhoejang juhgori 105
samo 87, 156
samo-gwan-dae 156
sam-ttwi 166
sang 29
sang-ah-hol 65
sang-bok 161, 166
sang-min 54
sangtu 30, 87
sanho 119
sarangbang 78
sarangchae 79
sat-gaht 138
Secret Garden 96
sedodae 87
Sejong, King 65, 76
seungmoo 143
shim-ui 84
shin(-bal) 26, 32, 134
ship-eejang-bok 62
sijo 168
sok-juksam 130
sok-sok-ot 130
soo 43
sookgosa 39

sool 120
Soonjong, King 69, 75, 76, 168
sseugae 130
su 102
suh-dang 62, 130
Sunduhk, Queen 22
sup 56
su-san-bok-hae 105
taegeuk 94
Taejo, King 46
taesahye 89, 136
Taewon-gun 60
tang-guhn 87
tanryong 156
tchang-ui 129
tchuhngsuk 99
tchun 142
tong-chima 180
toshi 127, 177
Toyotomi Hideyoshi 55
ttuljam 116, 159
ttwi 28, 195
uh-chowa 20
Unified Shilla, The 35
unmunsa 39
wang 142
wang-ja muni 30
wonhwa 146
wonsam 71, 100, 105
wonyugwan 65, 66
yaebok 130
yang 94
yangban 54
yang-dan 42
yang-mal 177
Yi Dynasty, The 54
Yi Song-gye 51, 54
Yi Sun-sin 55
yin 94
yo 20
yong-an 65
yong-bo 76
yong-jam 71
Yongjo, King 113
yongmun-sa 39
yong-po 65
yonjichuhb 123
yoohye 103
yosun-tchupli 52
Young-Wang 69
yum-jool 142
yunhwakwan 142

Photo Credit

Choi Chun-il   p187 (bottom)
Chung Soo-mi   p143, 144, 145
Hong Kyong-pyo   p197, 198 (L), 199 (L)
Debbie Kim   p50, 128 (L), Book back cover
Kim Hyung-jun   p173, 187 (above, R)
Kim Woo-suk   p42, 172
Ko Chang-soo   p118
Ko Jae-young   p49, 90 (bottom), 92 (L)
Koo Bohn-chang   p153, 155 (bottom)
Lee Chang-nam   p116, 175
Lee Jae-gil   Book front cover foreground, p156, 202, 203, 204, 205
Lee Man-hong   p193
Margaret McCollough   p62, 82, 83, 84, 132, 134, 177, 178, 182, 184, 188, 189
Min Sang-jun   p42, 129, 179
Noh Hyo-woon   Title page foreground
Michael O'Brien   p161, 162, 163, 164, 165, 186
Kazou Ohishi   p198 (R), 199 (R), 200, 201
Cynthia Tennent Sohn   p56
Park Sang-hun   p176
Suh Jai-sik   p125
Ella Yang   (Background photos) Front cover, Title page, p61, 128 (R), 160
Yoon Soo-jong   p185 (above), 187 (above, L)

Right Way of Tying *Goreum*

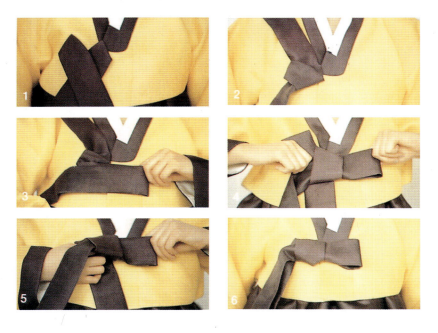

1. Tie shorter one above the longer one.
2. By making triangular form as the shorter one is pulled up under the longer one.
3. Fold the longer one above the triangular form, and tie by the shorter one going through the triangle.
4. Arrange firmly by pulling both *goreum* making 3-5 cm long head of tie.
5. Readjust making it firmly tied and right size.
6. Corrected *goreum*.
7. To keep it correctly tied, frequent adjusting is needed.